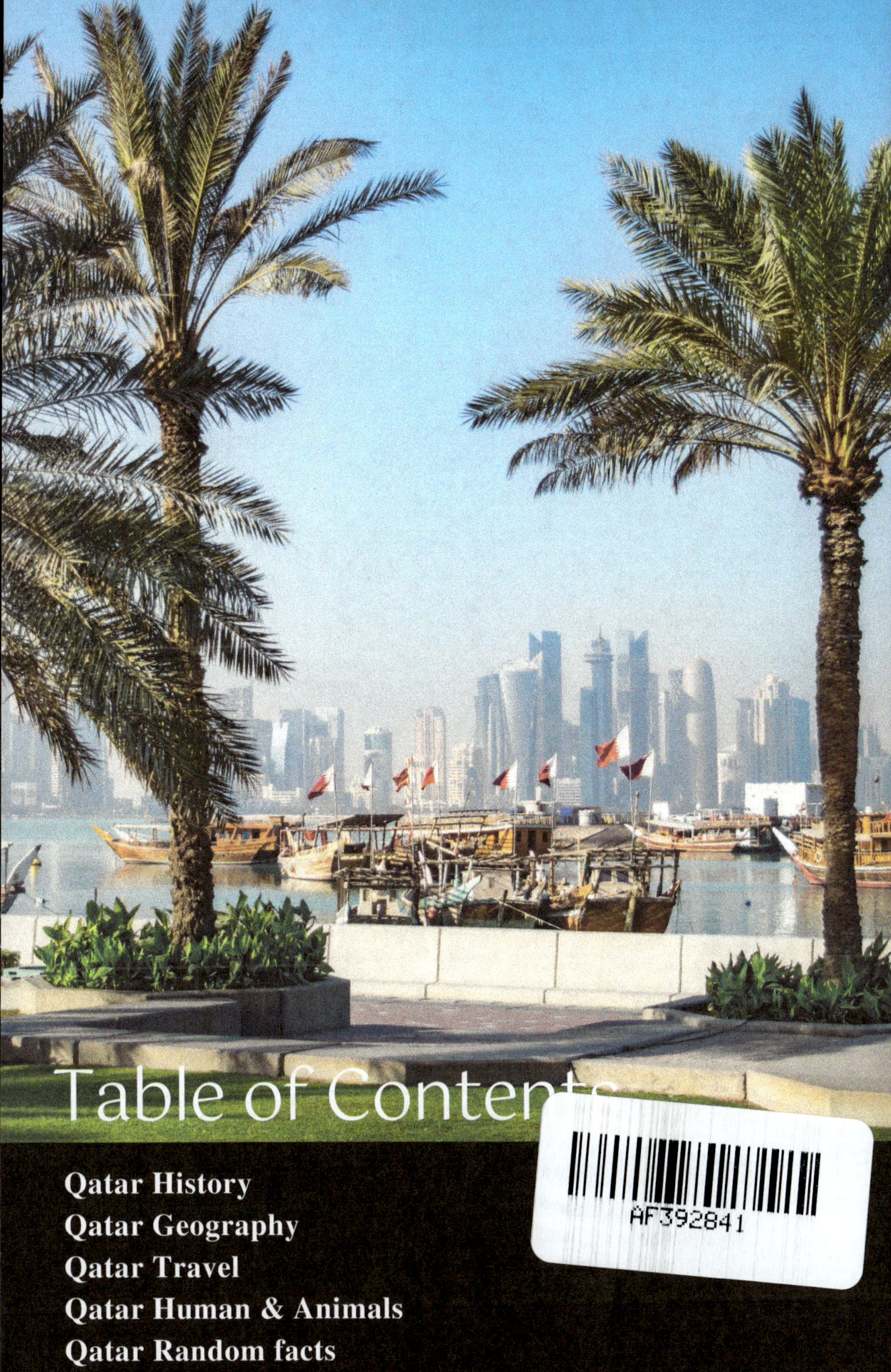

Table of Contents

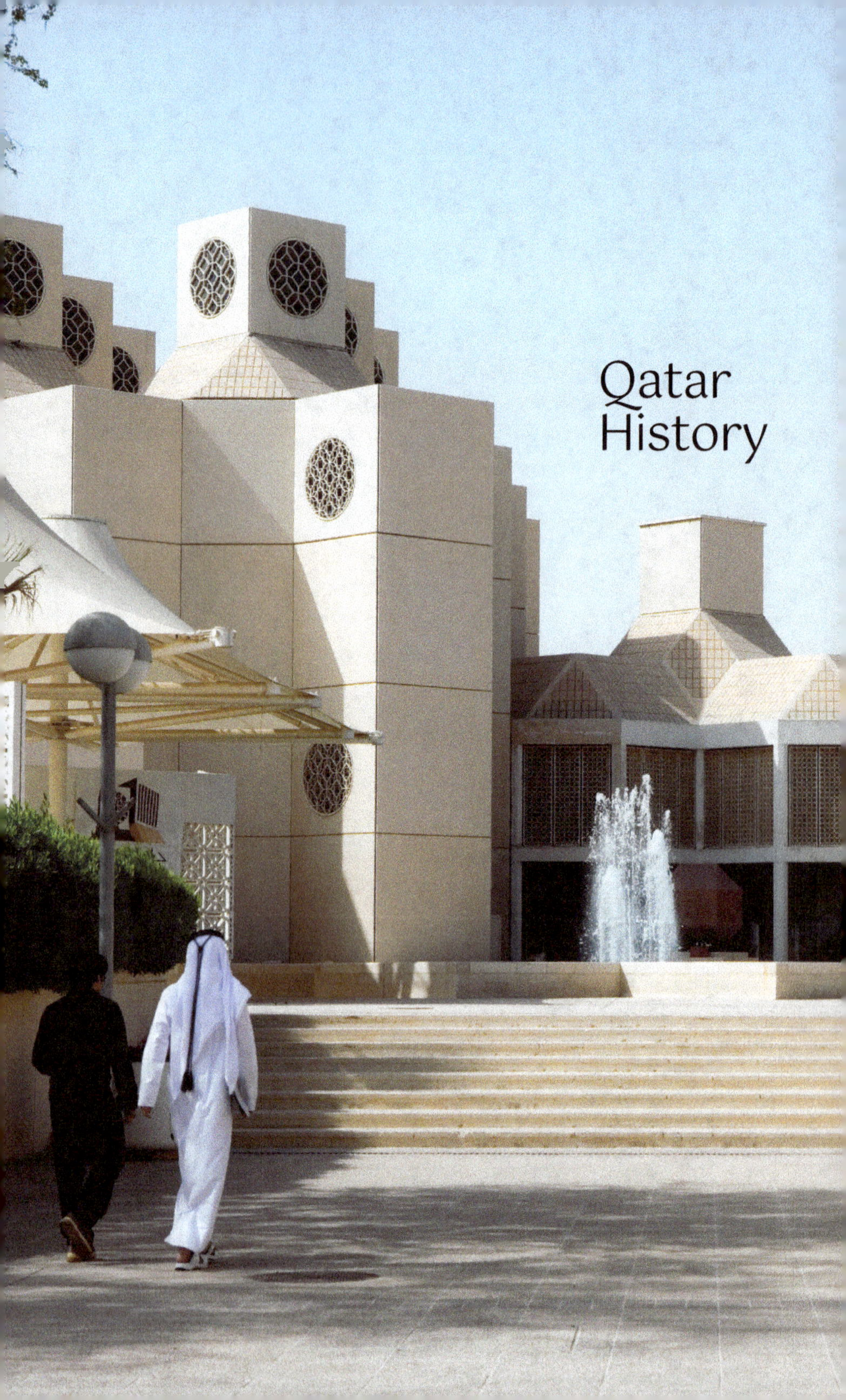
Qatar
History

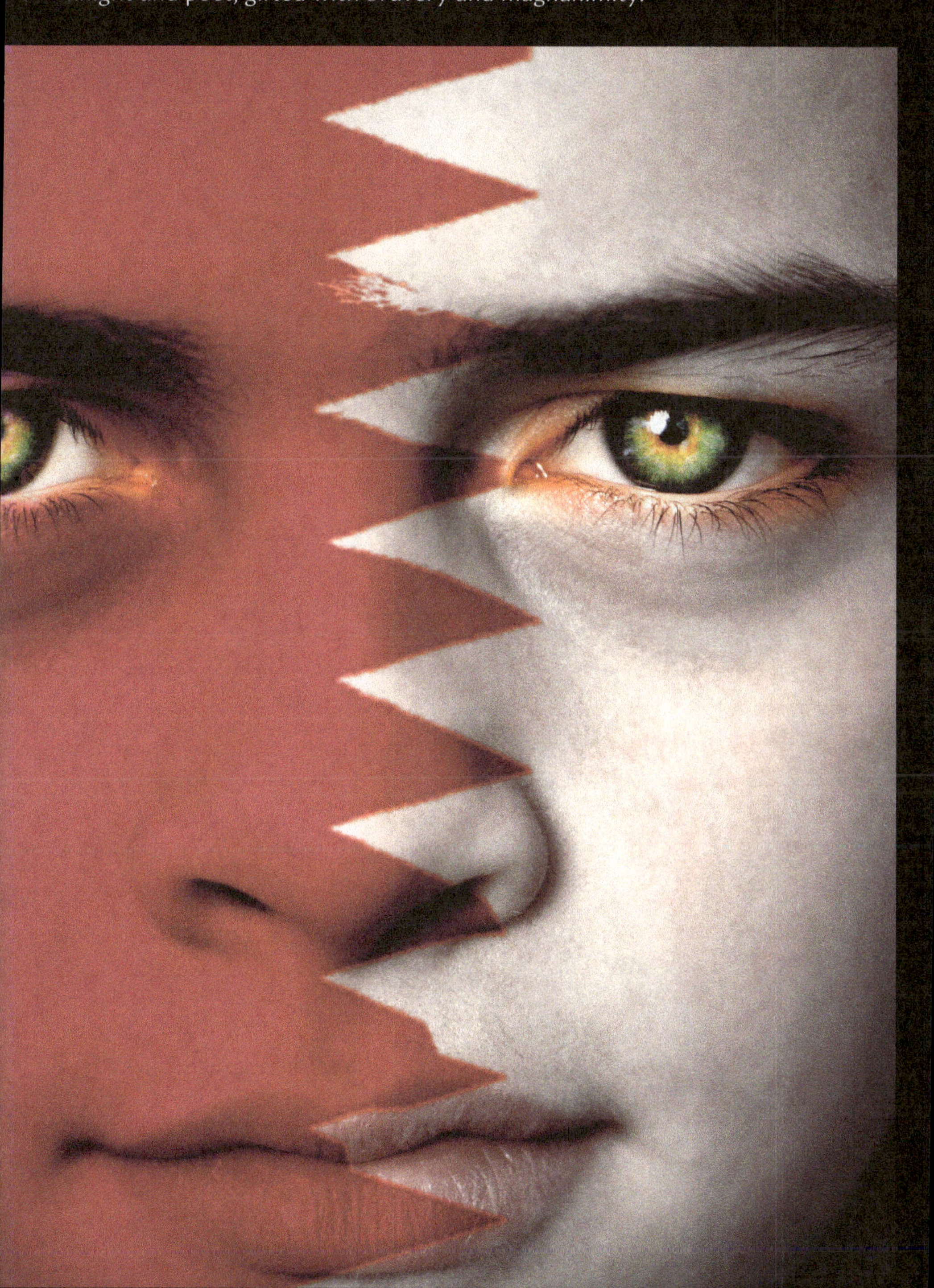

FOUNDER
The State of Qatar was established by Sheikh Jassim Bin Mohammed Bin Thani. a leader in the military, judge and scholar, knight and poet, gifted with bravery and magnanimity.

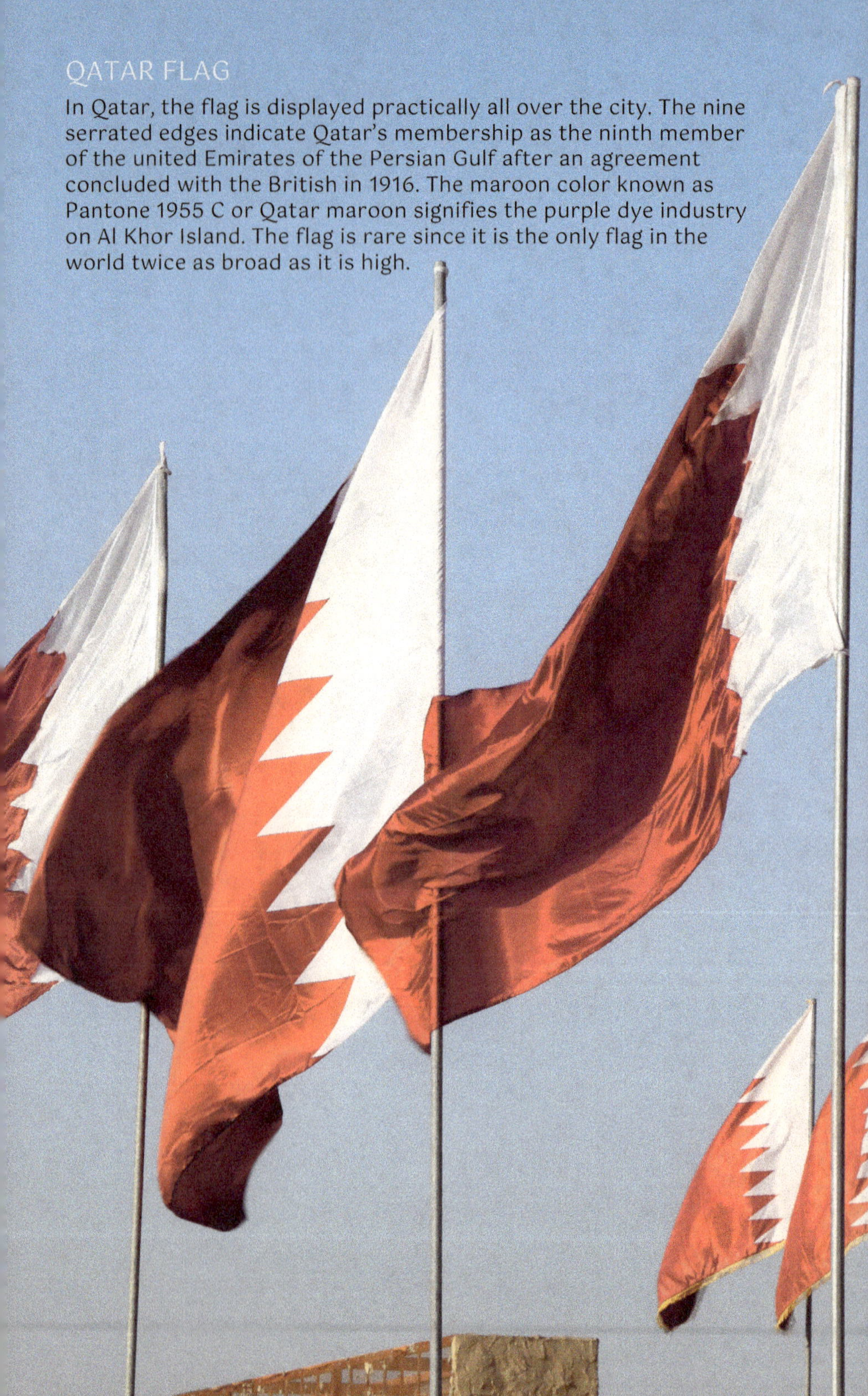

QATAR FLAG
In Qatar, the flag is displayed practically all over the city. The nine serrated edges indicate Qatar's membership as the ninth member of the united Emirates of the Persian Gulf after an agreement concluded with the British in 1916. The maroon color known as Pantone 1955 C or Qatar maroon signifies the purple dye industry on Al Khor Island. The flag is rare since it is the only flag in the world twice as broad as it is high.

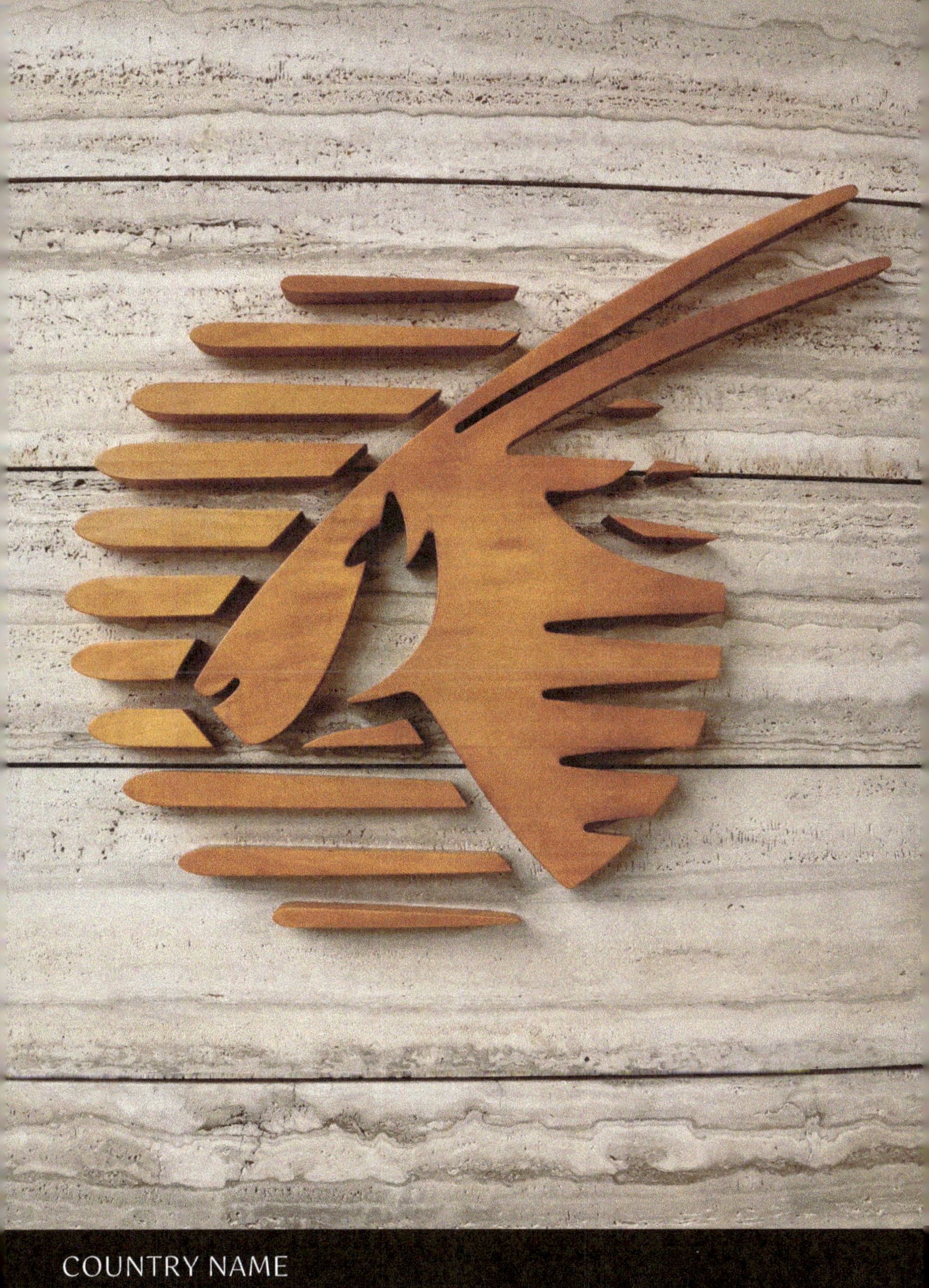

COUNTRY NAME

The name Qatar goes back to 50AD. In the mid-first century, the Roman writer
Pliny the Elder referred to the people of what is now Qatar as 'Catharrei'. The
name has gone through various changes since then. Up to the 18th century, the
name Catara was used before Katara became the more popular spelling. More
versions developed such Katr, Kattar, and Guttur which were rapidly embraced as

PEARL DIVING TO OIL

Pearl diving was a cornerstone of the Qatari economy for thousands of years, and is valued as a significant aspect of the country's culture. That all changed in the 1920s, when Japan started exporting cultivated pearls, and the market was saturated. Qatar, like many nations in the Gulf area, stepped to oil, digging its first well in 1939, and exporting crude oil as early as 1949. More fields were identified in 1960, and again in 1970. Oil is now a big component of the economy, and Qatar is even home to the longest drilled oil well in the world, at 40,320 ft.

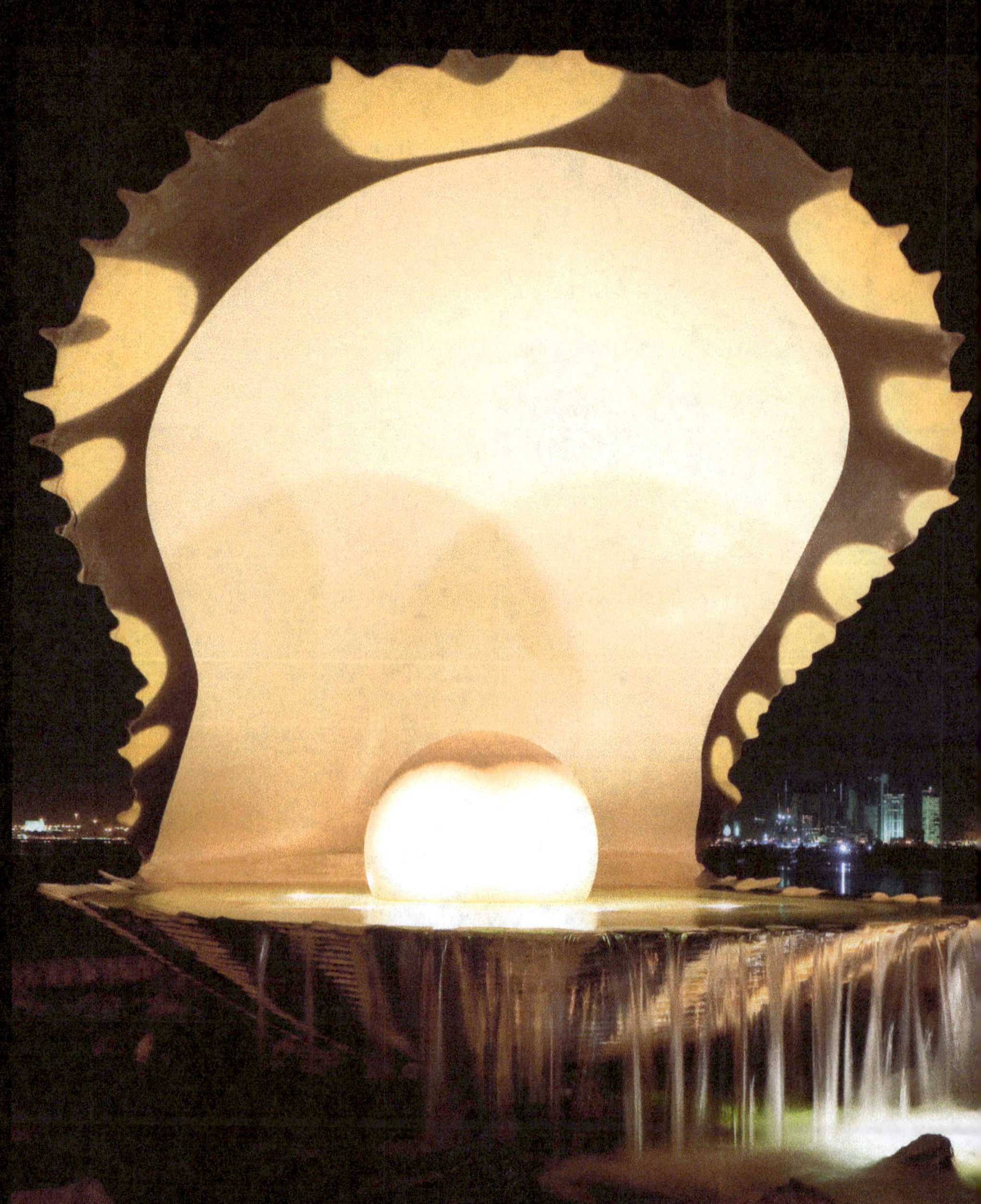

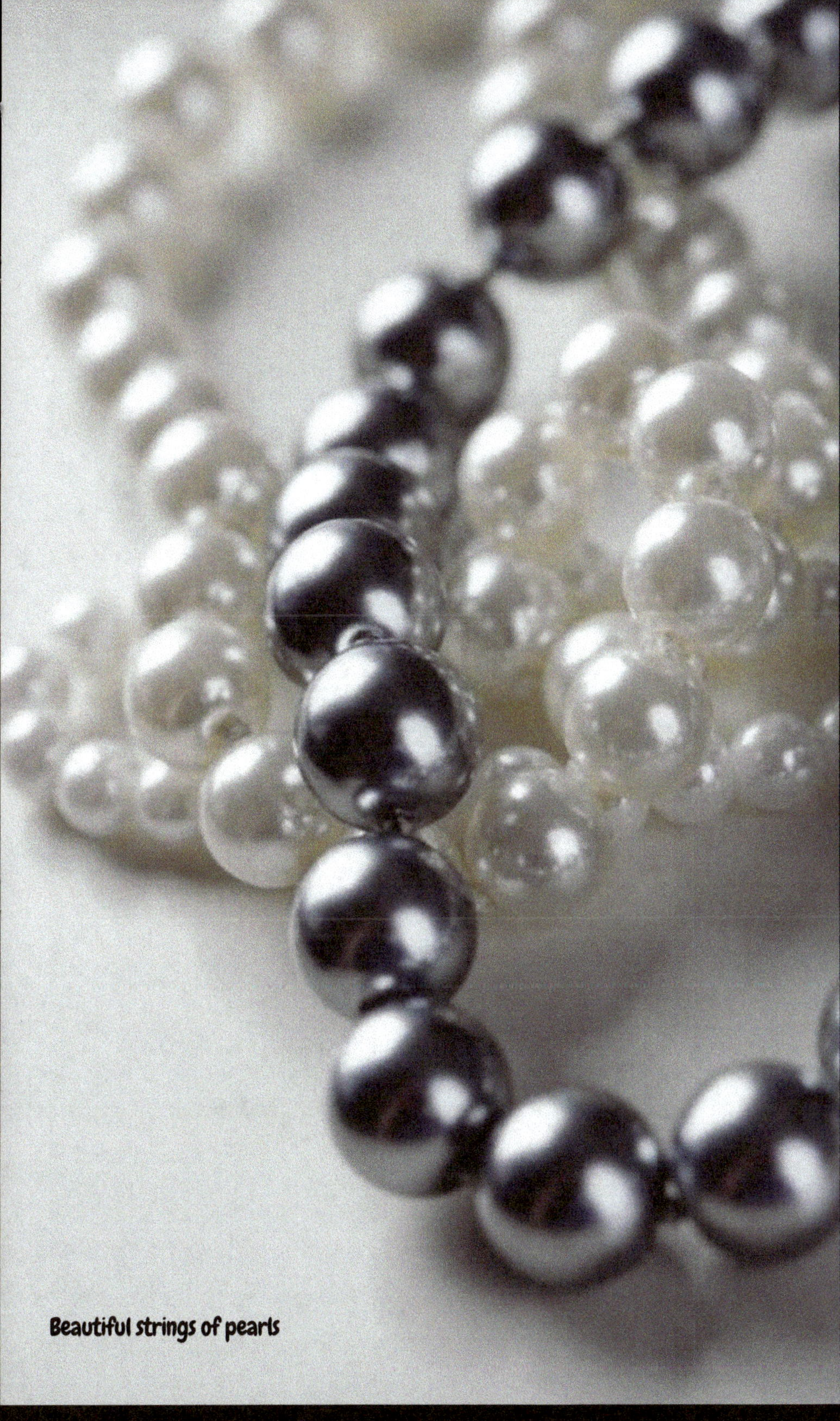
Beautiful strings of pearls

RULING FAMILY

Ruling families around the world have changed throughout history. Qatar's ruling family has been in power since 1868. The House of Thani, as the royal family is known, is the most powerful family in Qatar. The people are loyal to the royal family and have lived a wonderful life under them. The current Emir is Tamim bin Hamad Al Thani, who has ruled over the country since 2013.

FACTS ABOUT SHEIKH TAMIM

Sheikh Tamim bin Hamad Al Thani is the ruler of Qatar. He is the 10th richest member of royalty in the world, with a net worth of $2.1 billion. He owns the Paris Saint-Germain F.C. football club and has been called "the best sport personality in the Arab world".

RICHEST COUNTRY

Qatar is one of the richest countries in the world. According to the International Monetary Fund's 2020 predictions, Qatar's gross domestic product (GDP per capital is a stunning $138,910, placing it considerably ahead of Luxembourg's $112,045 in second place. Unsurprisingly, most of this income comes from petroleum and natural gas, which account for more than 60 percent of GDP.

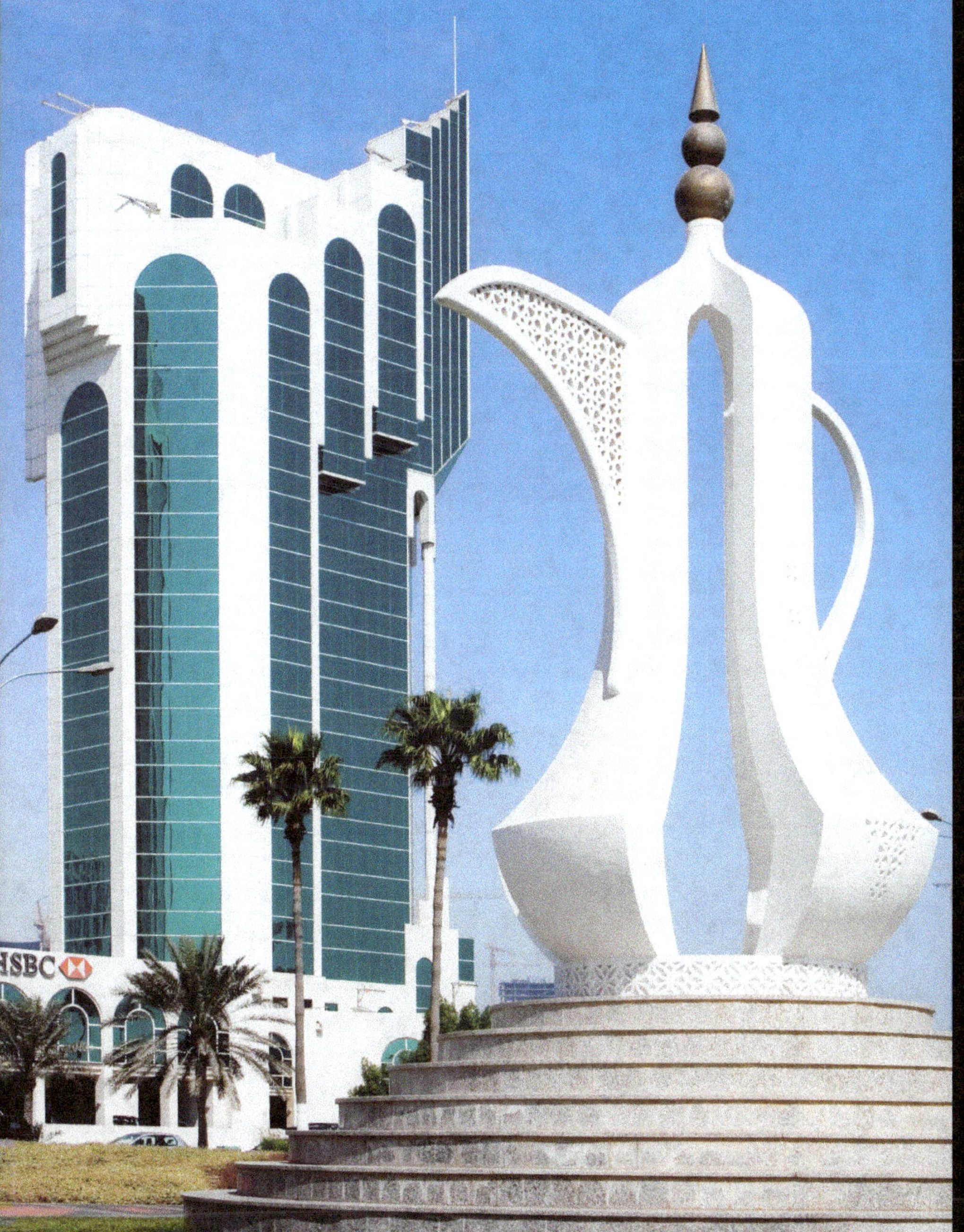

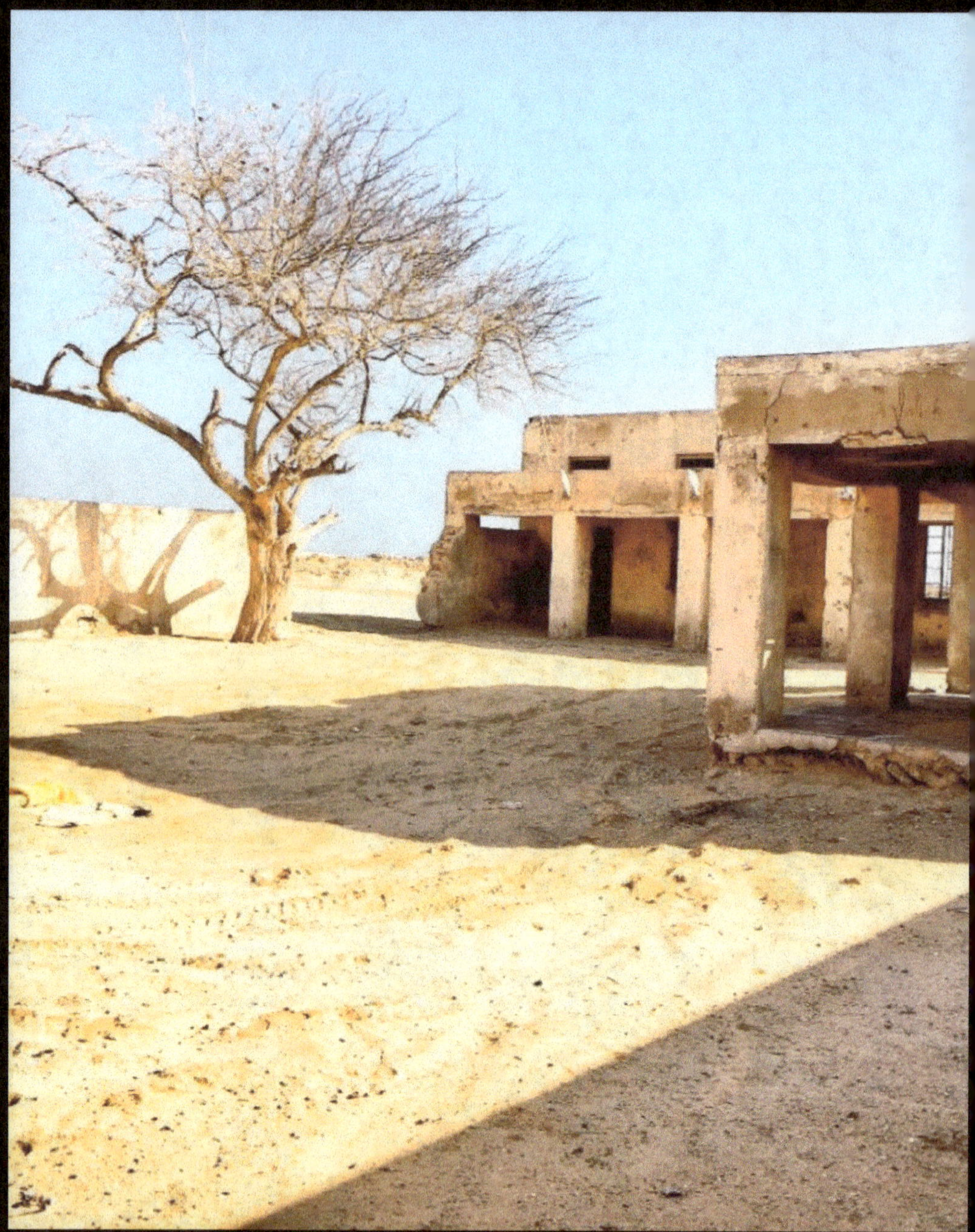

FIRST SCHOOL

The emir of Qatar founded Islah al-Mohammadiyeh, the first official school in the country, in Doha in 1949. There were 50 students enrolled and one educator working there. In its early years, it expanded quickly, and by 1950–1951, it was thought to have space for 240 students and 6 teachers.

FIRST HOSPITAL

The first hospital in Qatar was established by the American Mission in 1947, but Al Rumailah, the first public hospital, debuted in 1957 and is still in use today. Despite major renovations since its establishment, it continues to be Doha's oldest hospital.

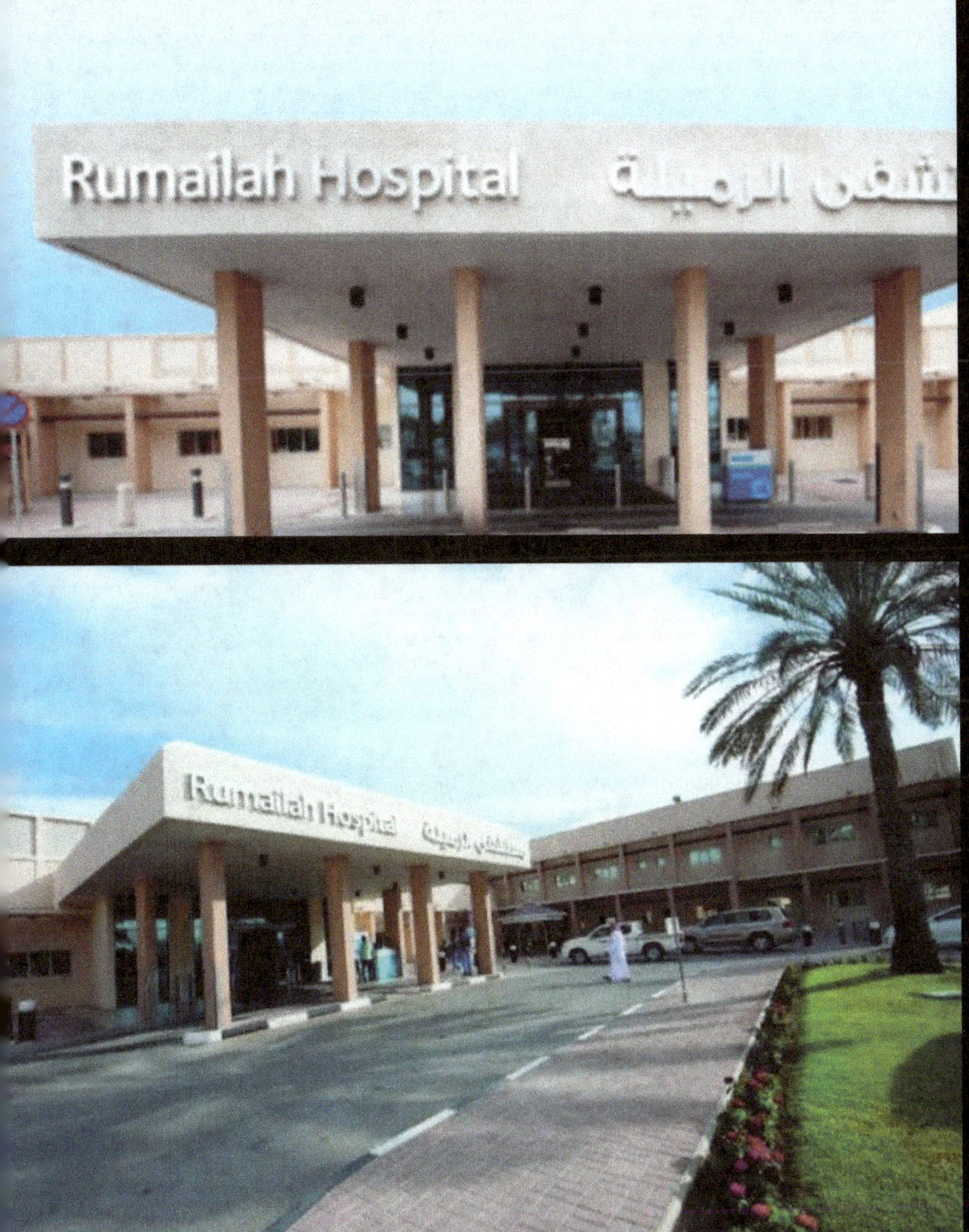

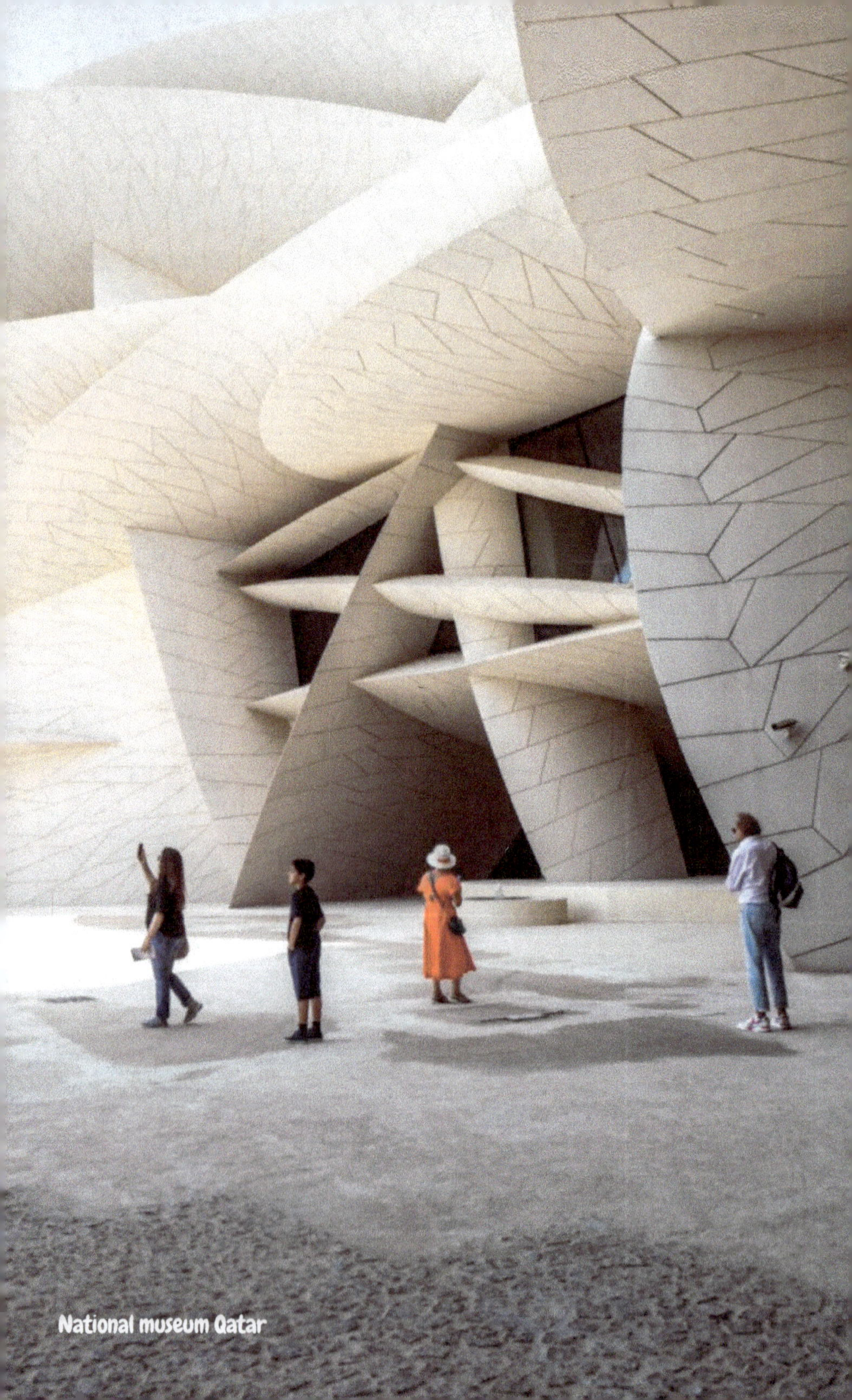
National museum Qatar

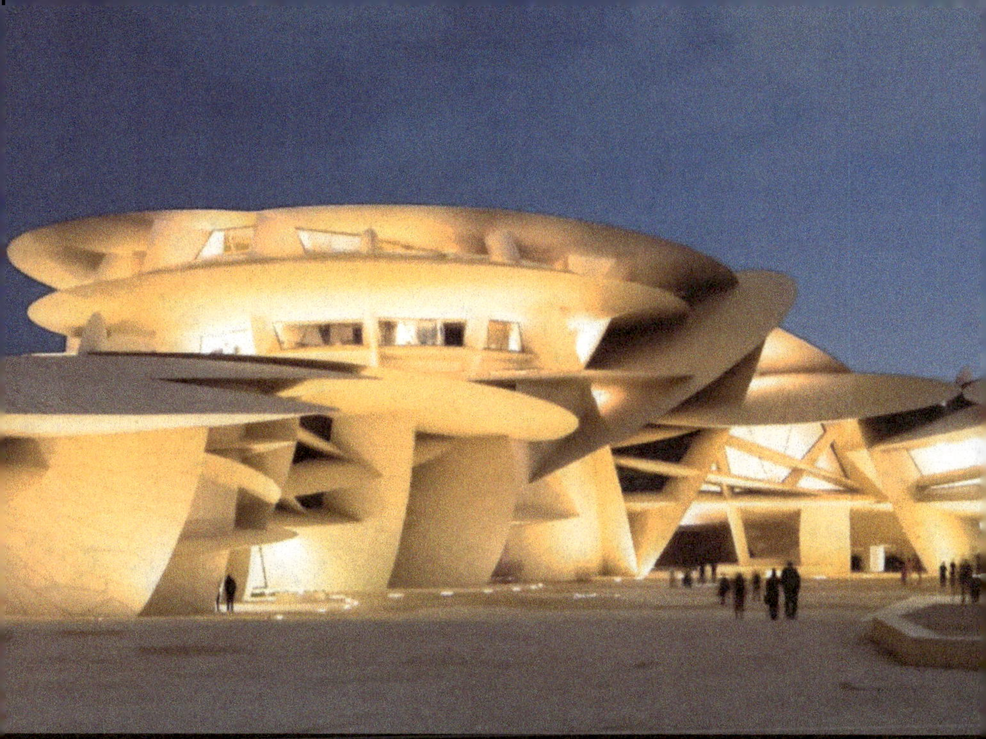

NATIONAL MUSEUM

In Doha, Qatar, there is a museum known as the National Museum of Qatar. On March 28, 2019, the modern building, which replaced the earlier one that had debuted in 1975, was made publicly accessible. The desert rose crystal, which can be found in Qatar, served as inspiration for the architect Jean Nouvel as he created the structure.

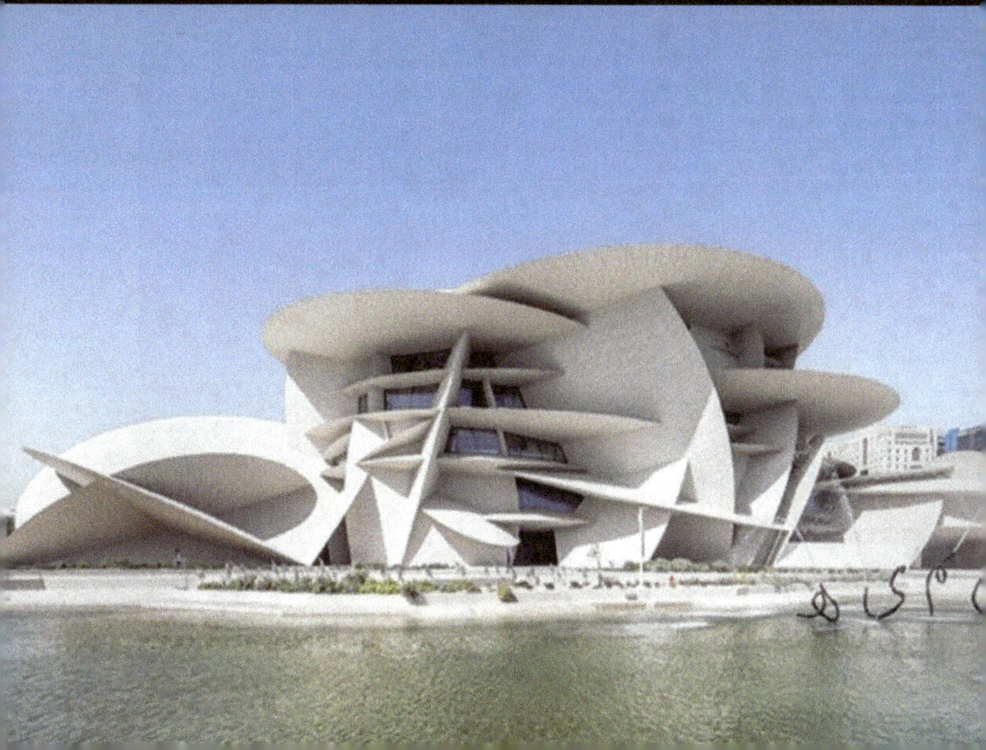

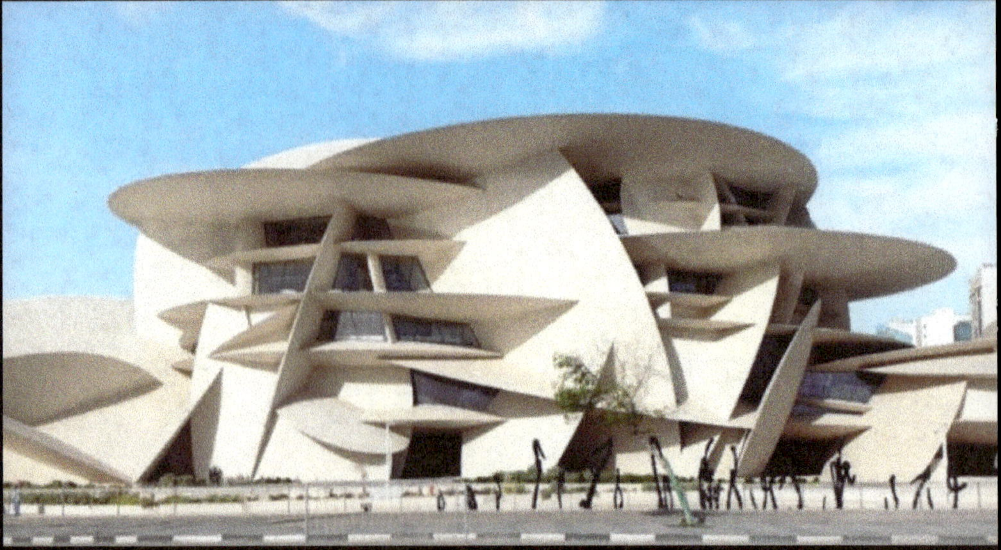

National museum Qatar

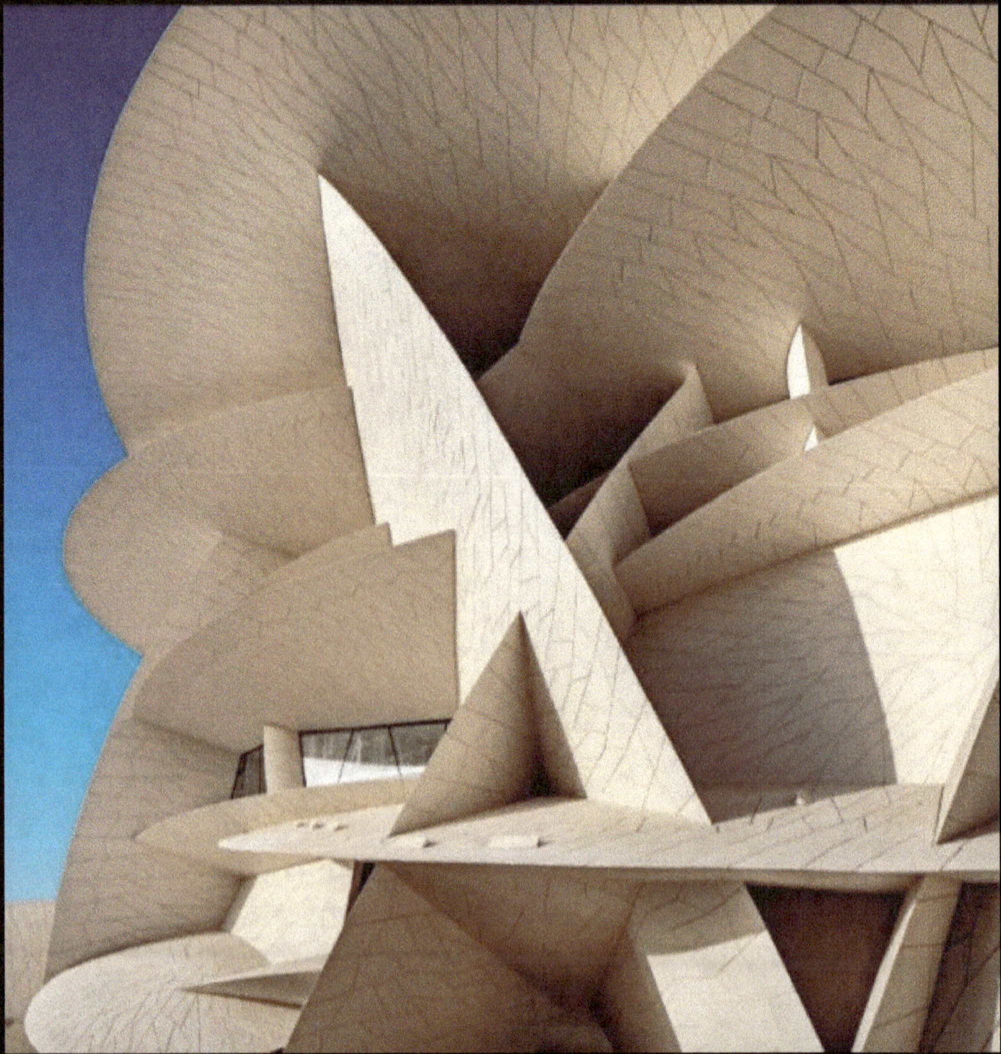

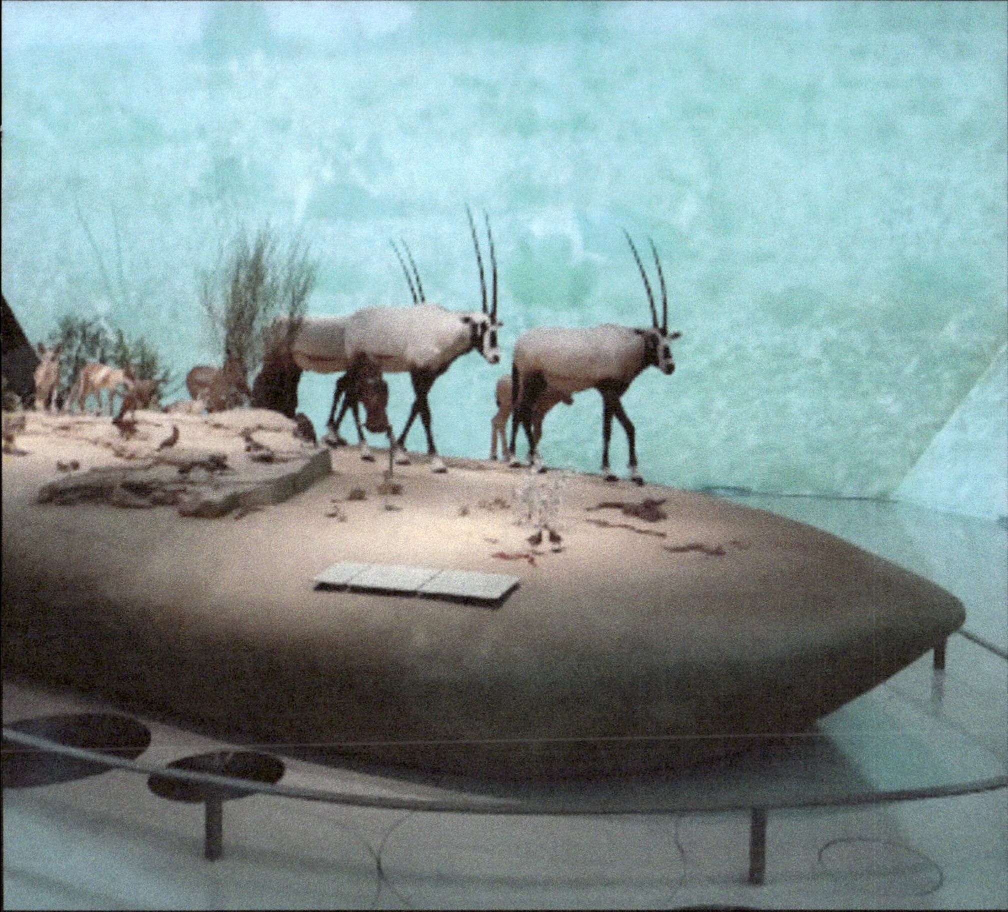

National museum Qatar

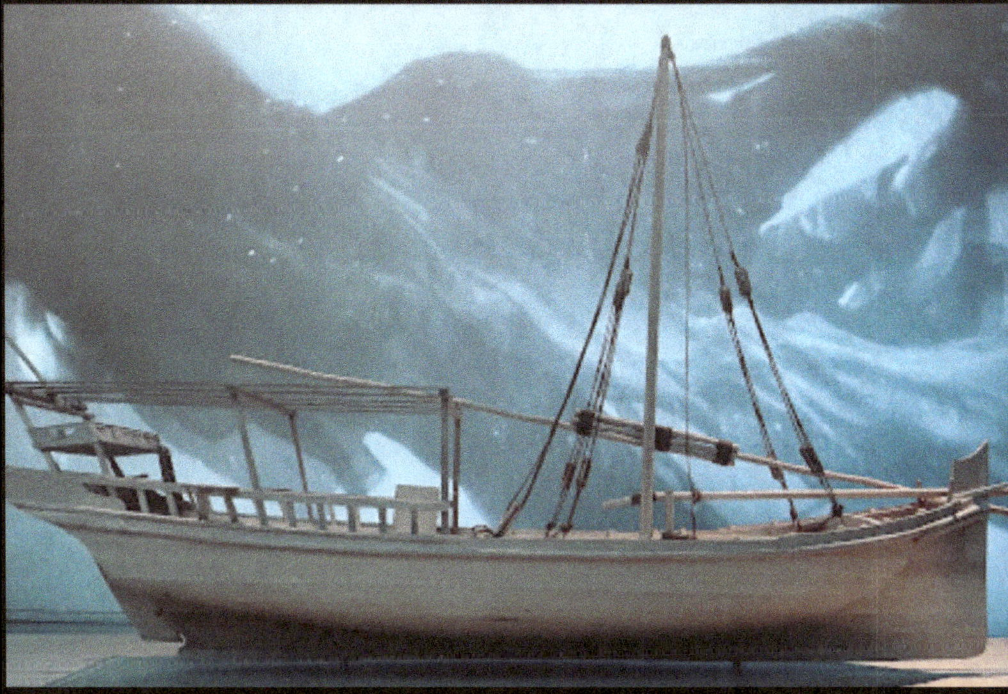

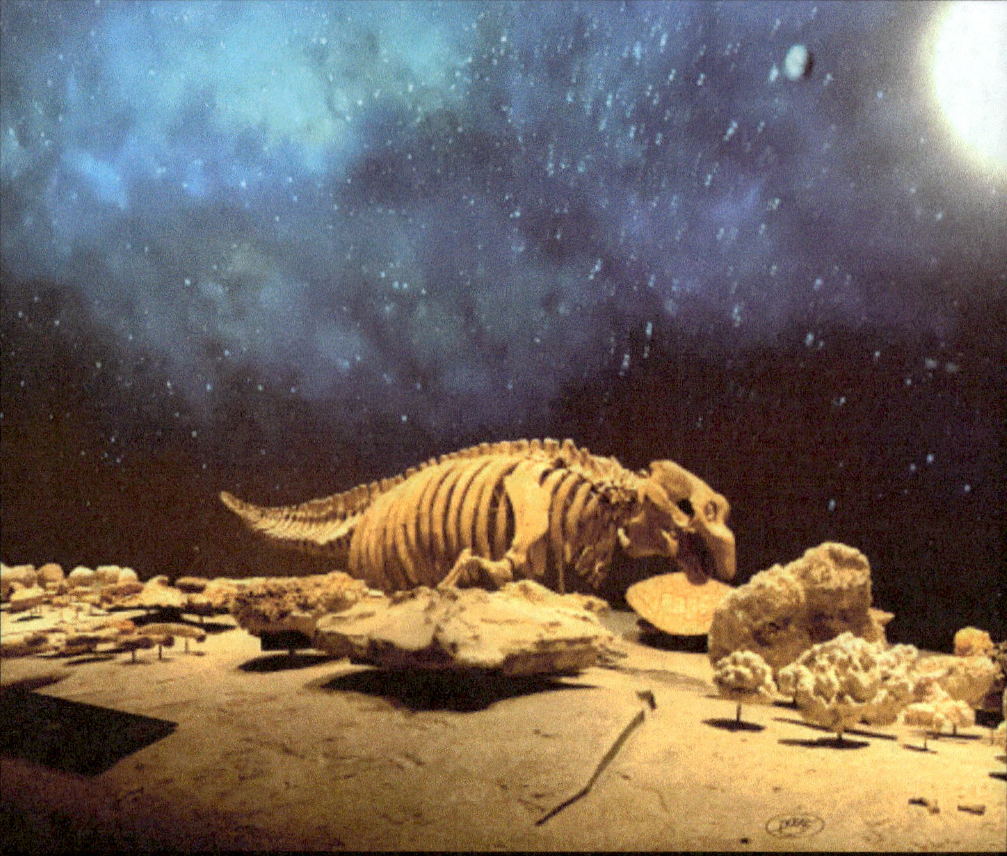

National museum Qatar

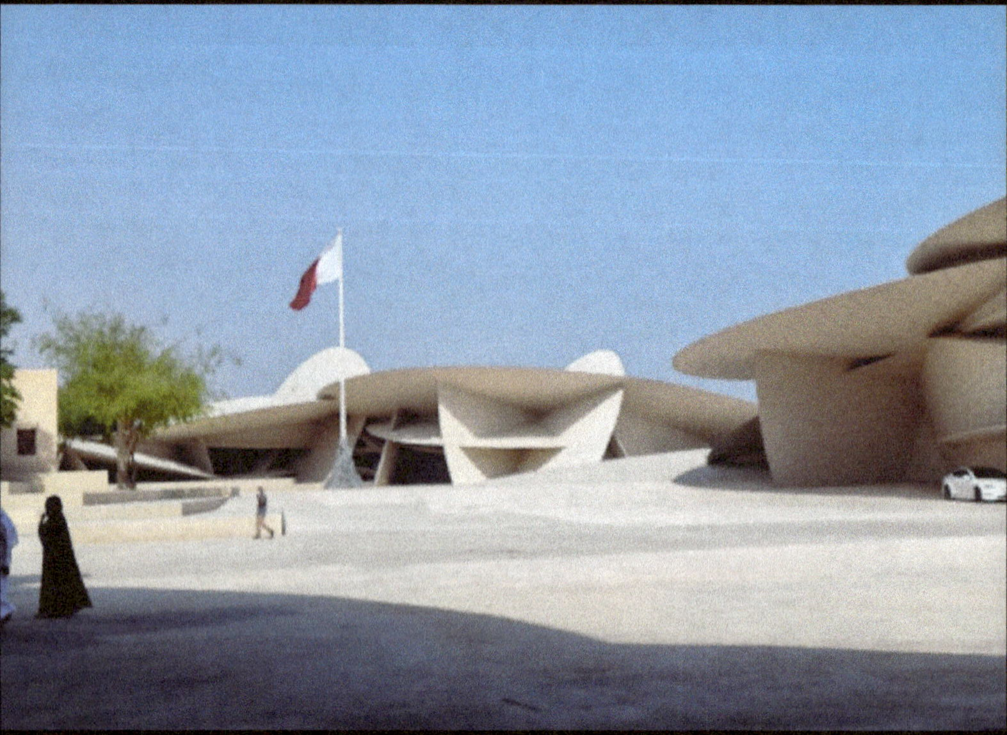

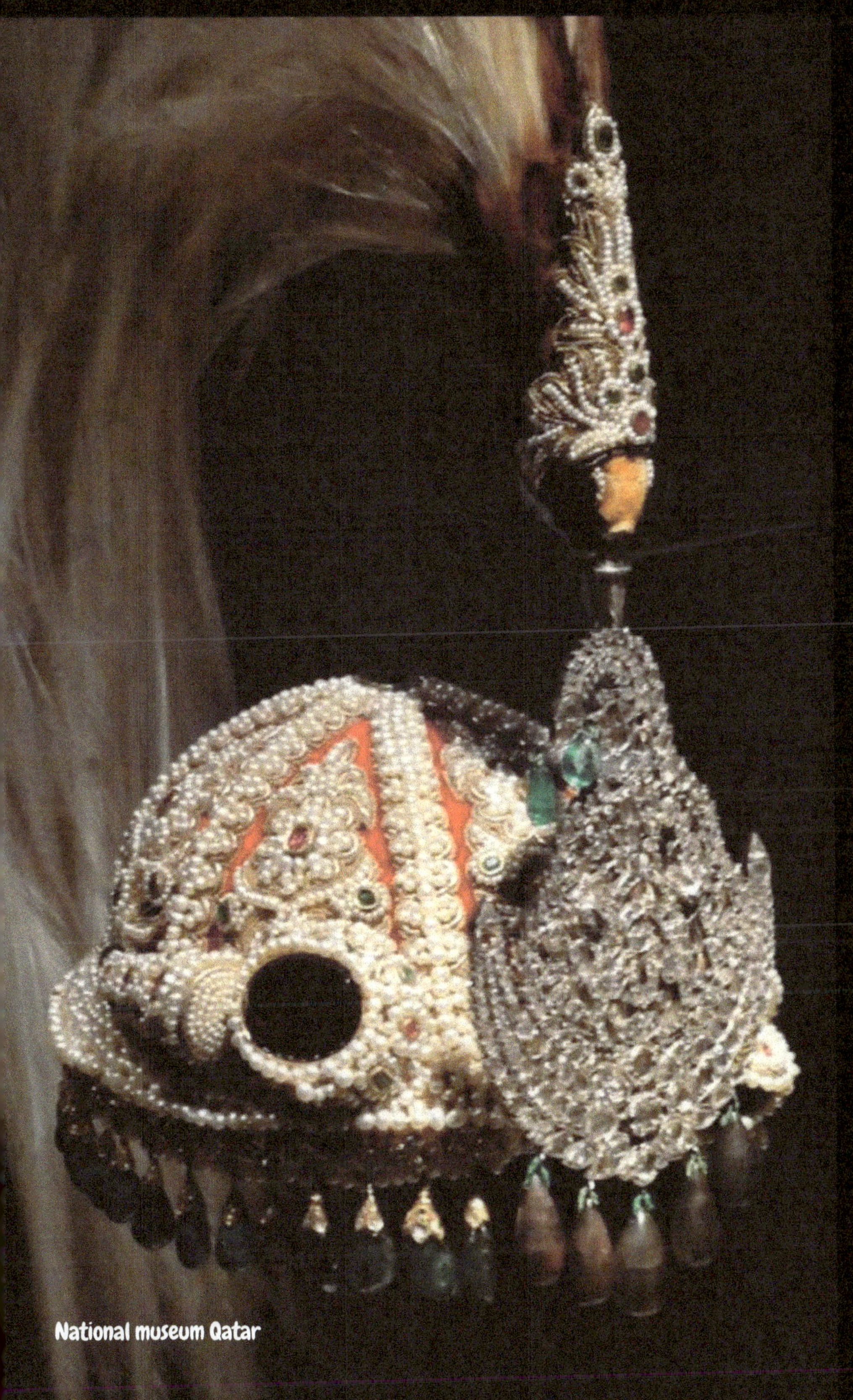
National museum Qatar

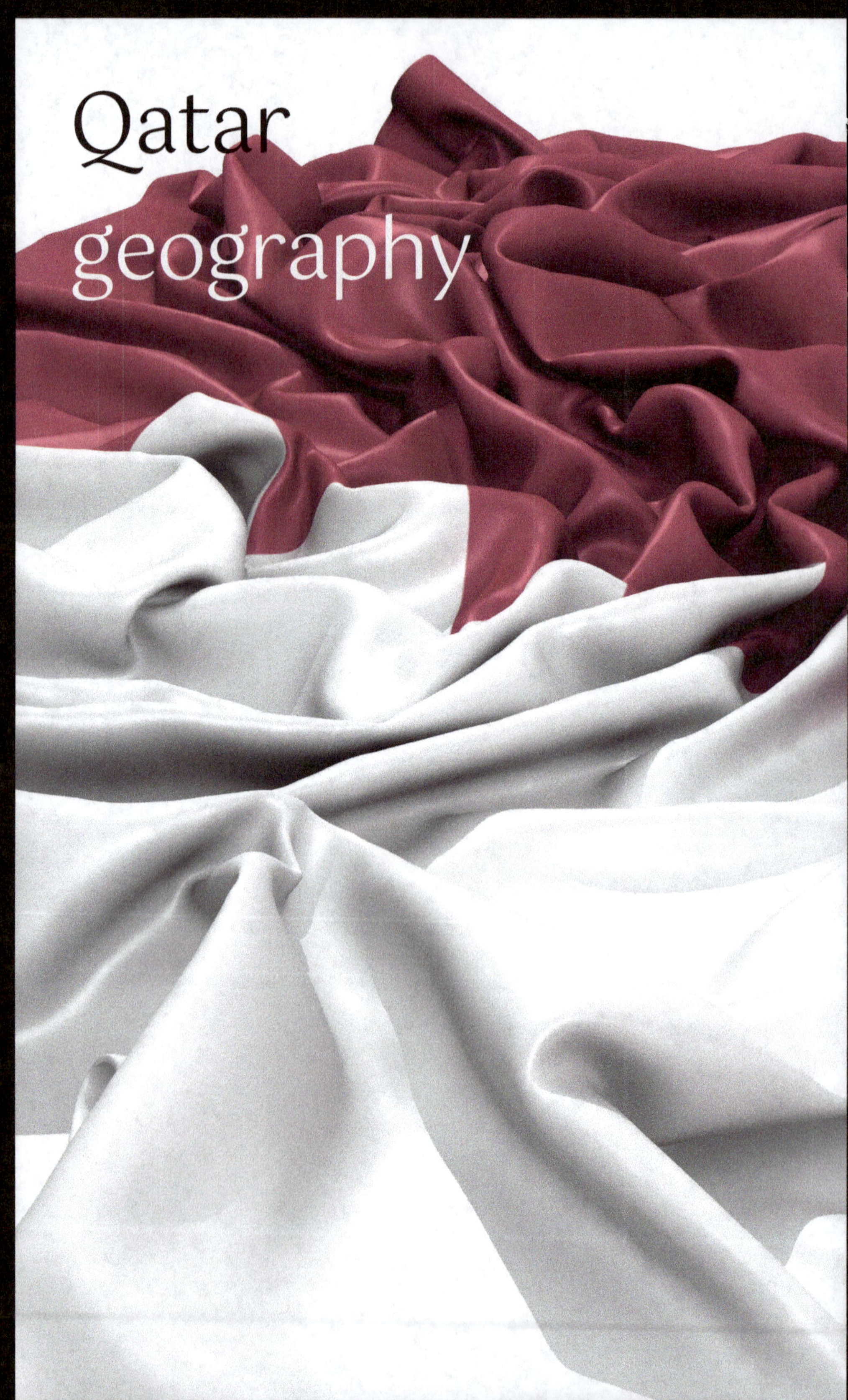
Qatar
geography

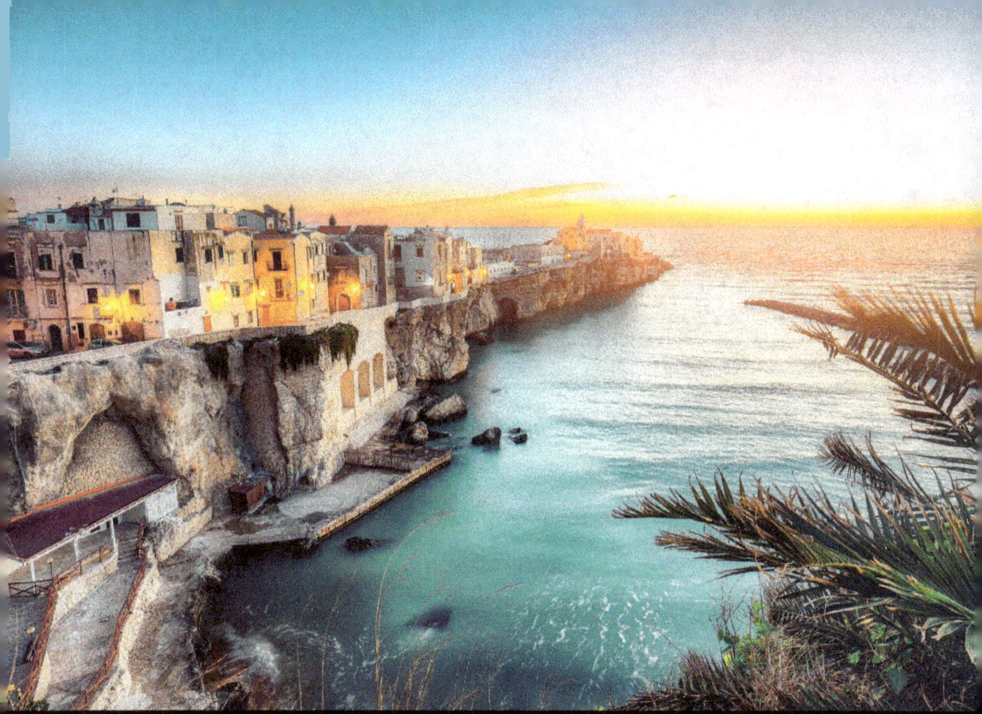

PENINSULA

Qatar has a coastline of 563 km
Qatar is a peninsula, which means it is surrounded by water on most of
its sides, giving it a lengthy coastline with a length of 563 km.

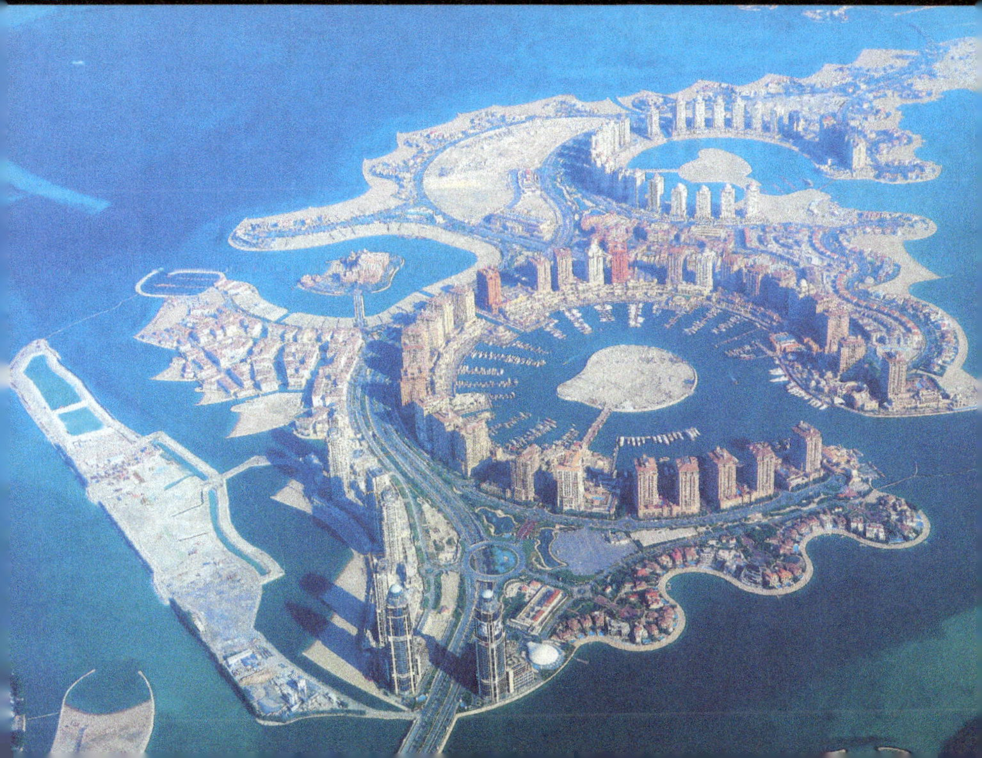

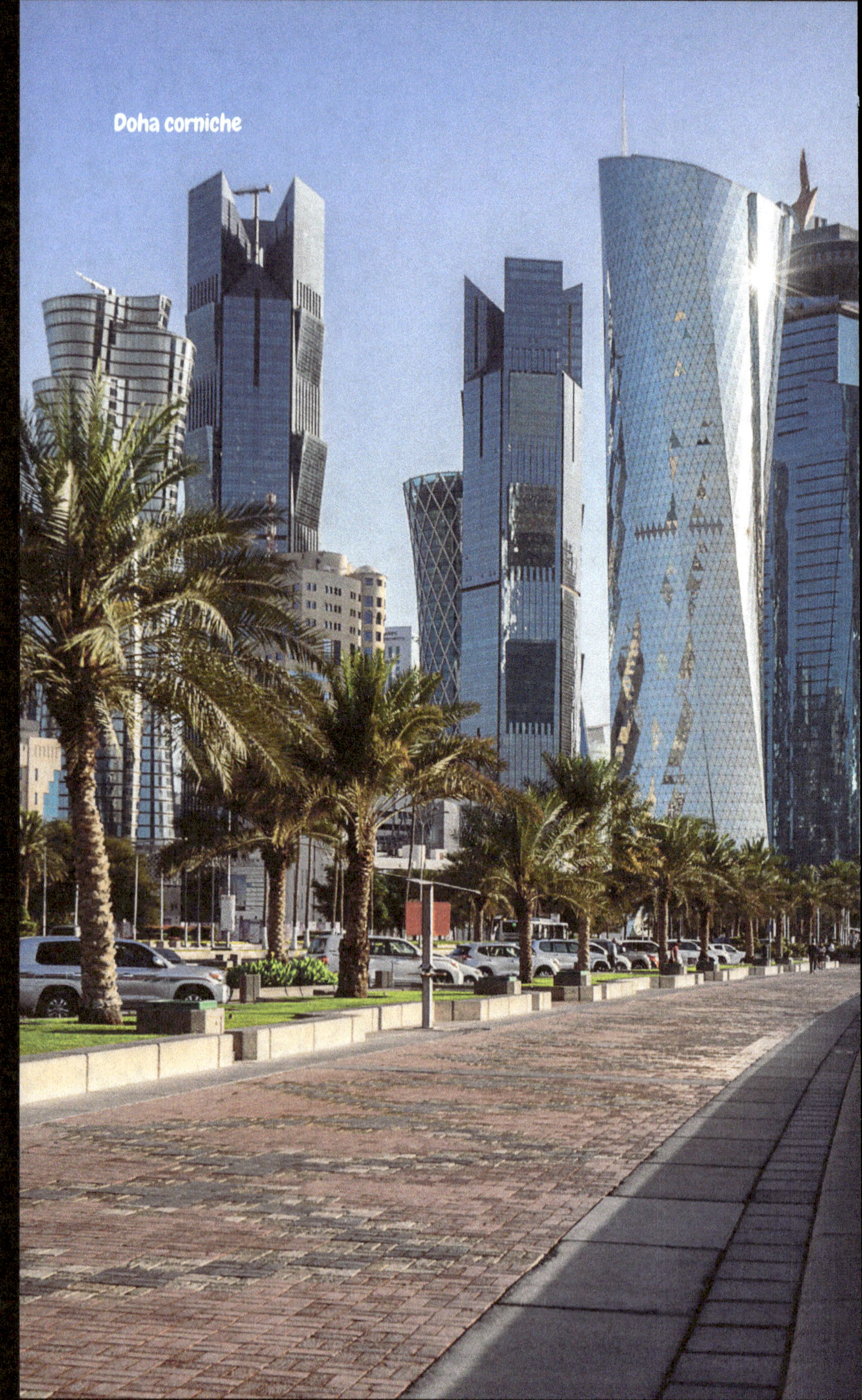
Doha corniche

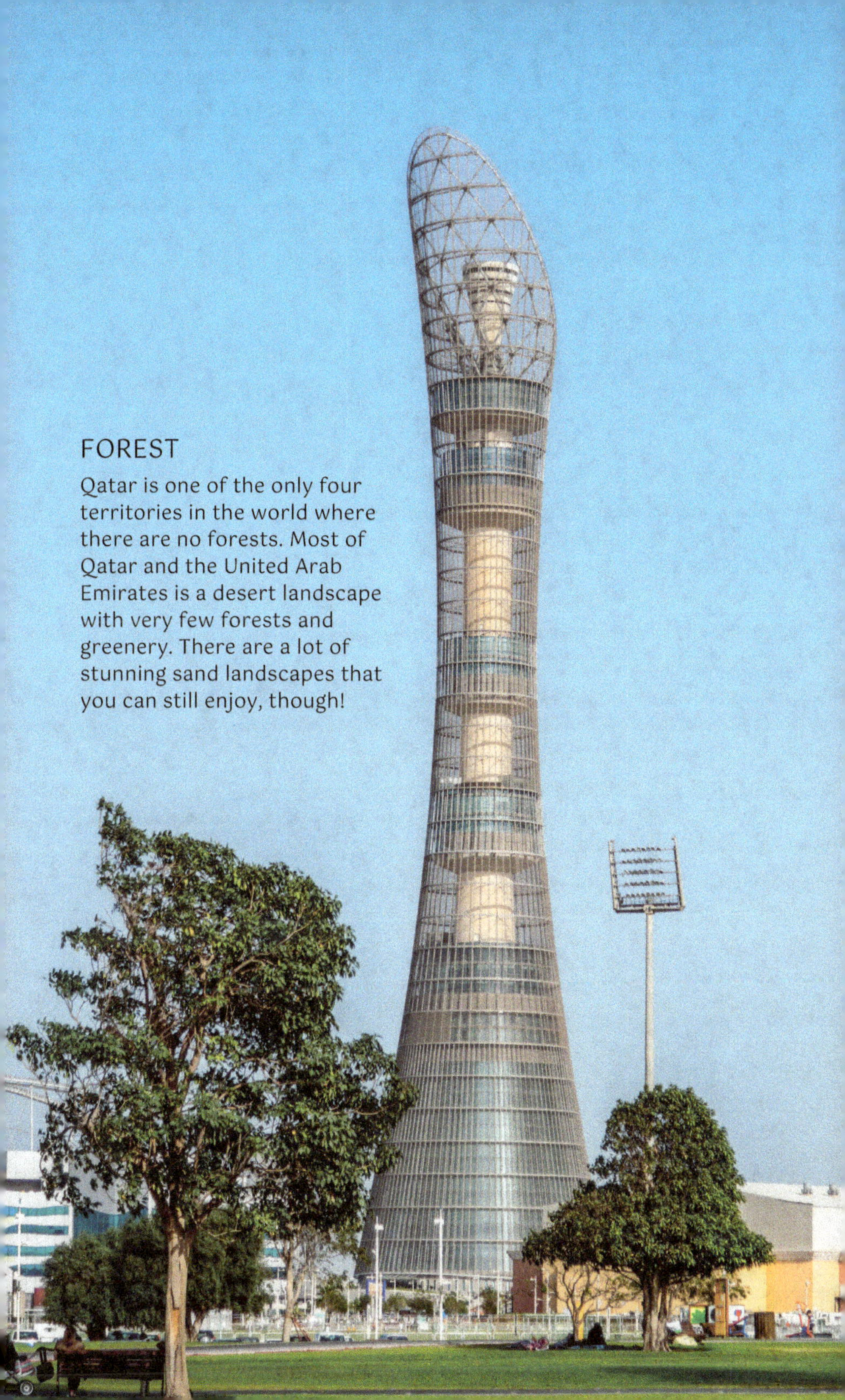

FOREST

Qatar is one of the only four territories in the world where there are no forests. Most of Qatar and the United Arab Emirates is a desert landscape with very few forests and greenery. There are a lot of stunning sand landscapes that you can still enjoy, though!

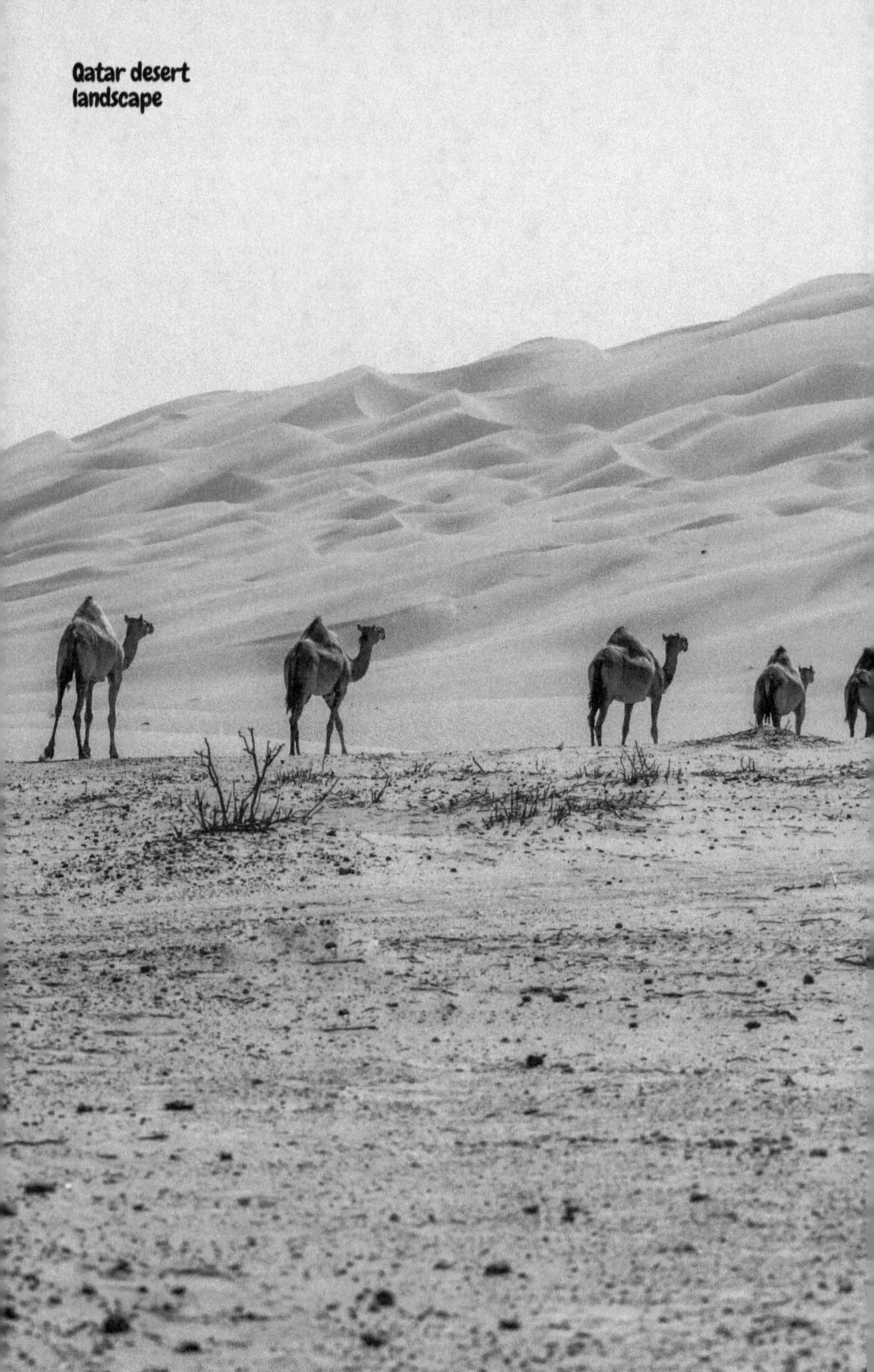
Qatar desert
landscape

FLAT COUNTRY

Qatar is the second flattest country in the world, after the Maldives. It has an average elevation of 91.9 ft, with the highest height of 338 ft. The country is lots of flat expanses, and they are lovely to look at. There are no hills or cliffs, It's excellent news for cyclists and runners, poor news for hikers.

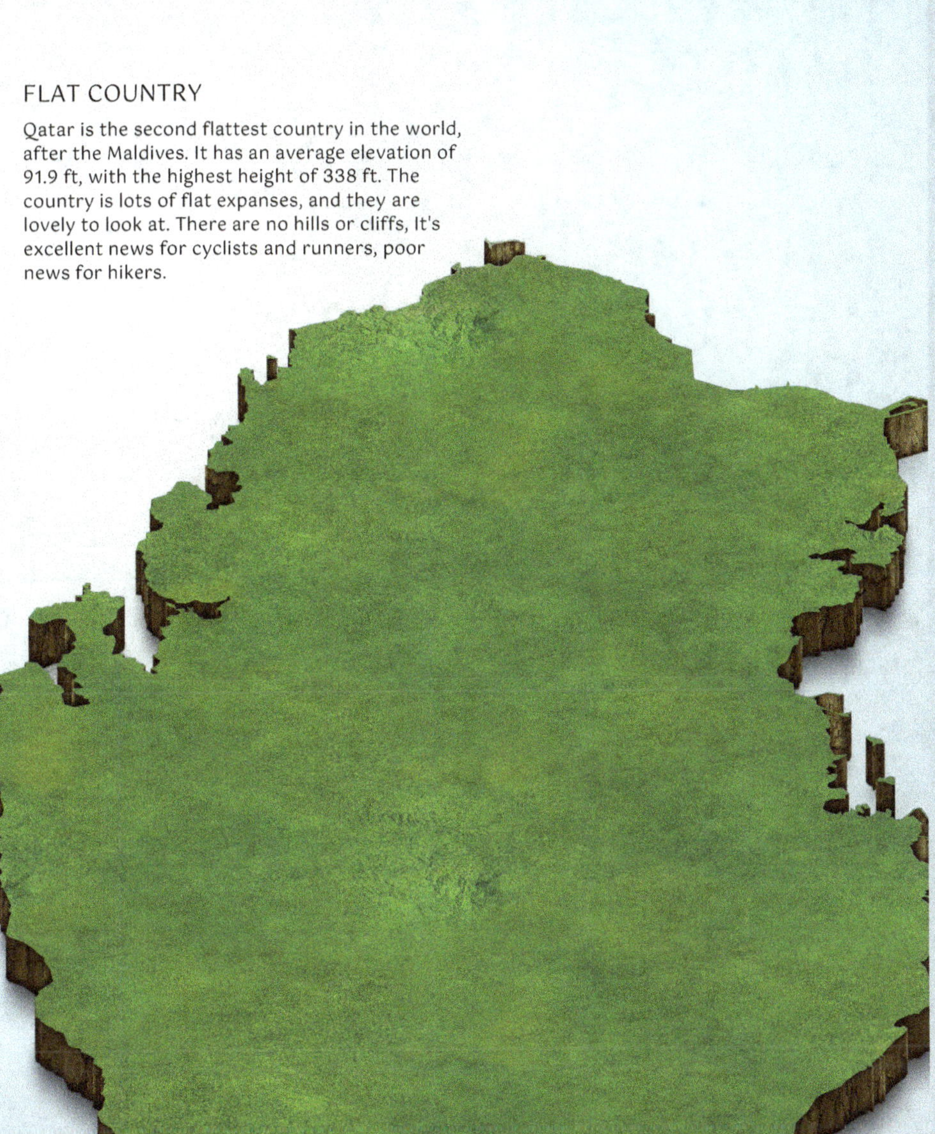

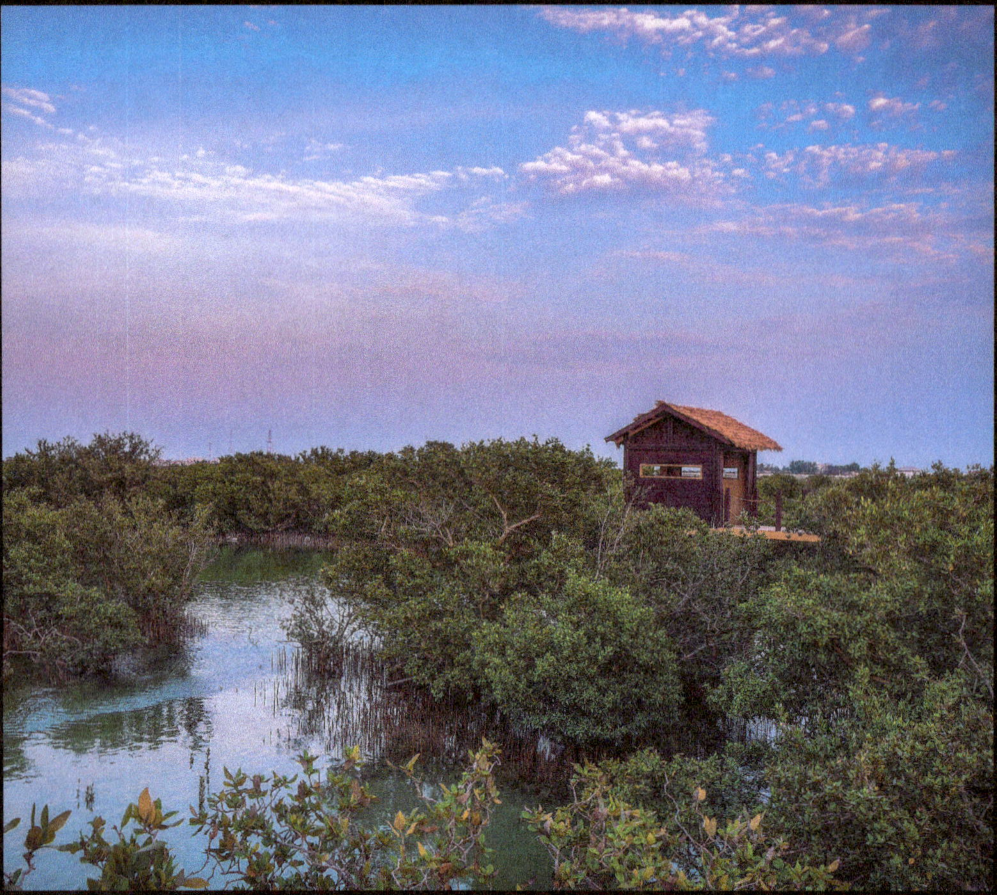

PURPLE ISLAND

Al Khor Island is one of the most beautiful and popular tourist destinations in Qatar. There have been discoveries of items from the second millennium BC, and the island is called the Purple Island due to the dye production that happens here. The inhabitants of Al Khor are also known for being the first to make purple dye out of shellfish.

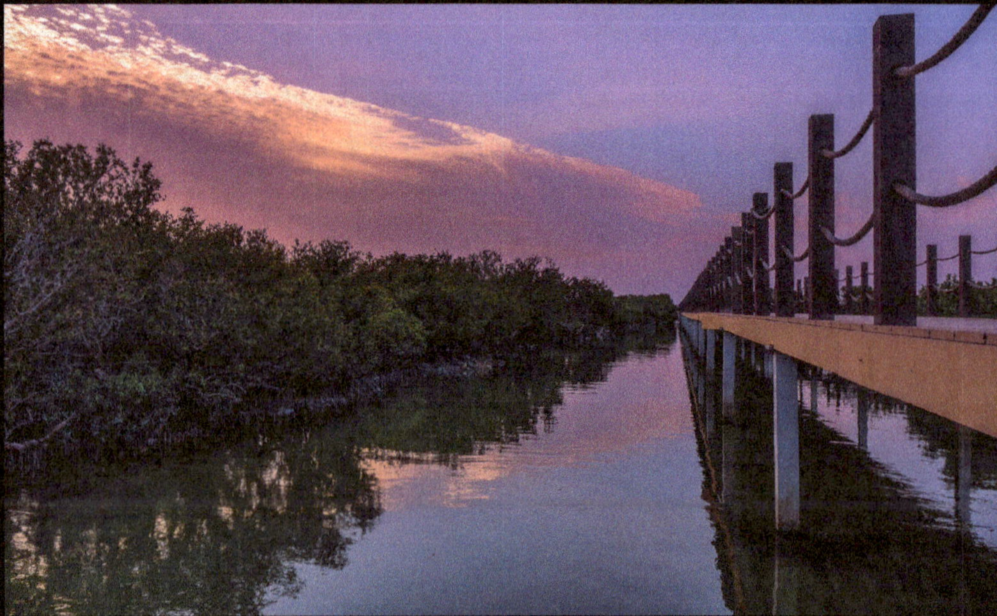

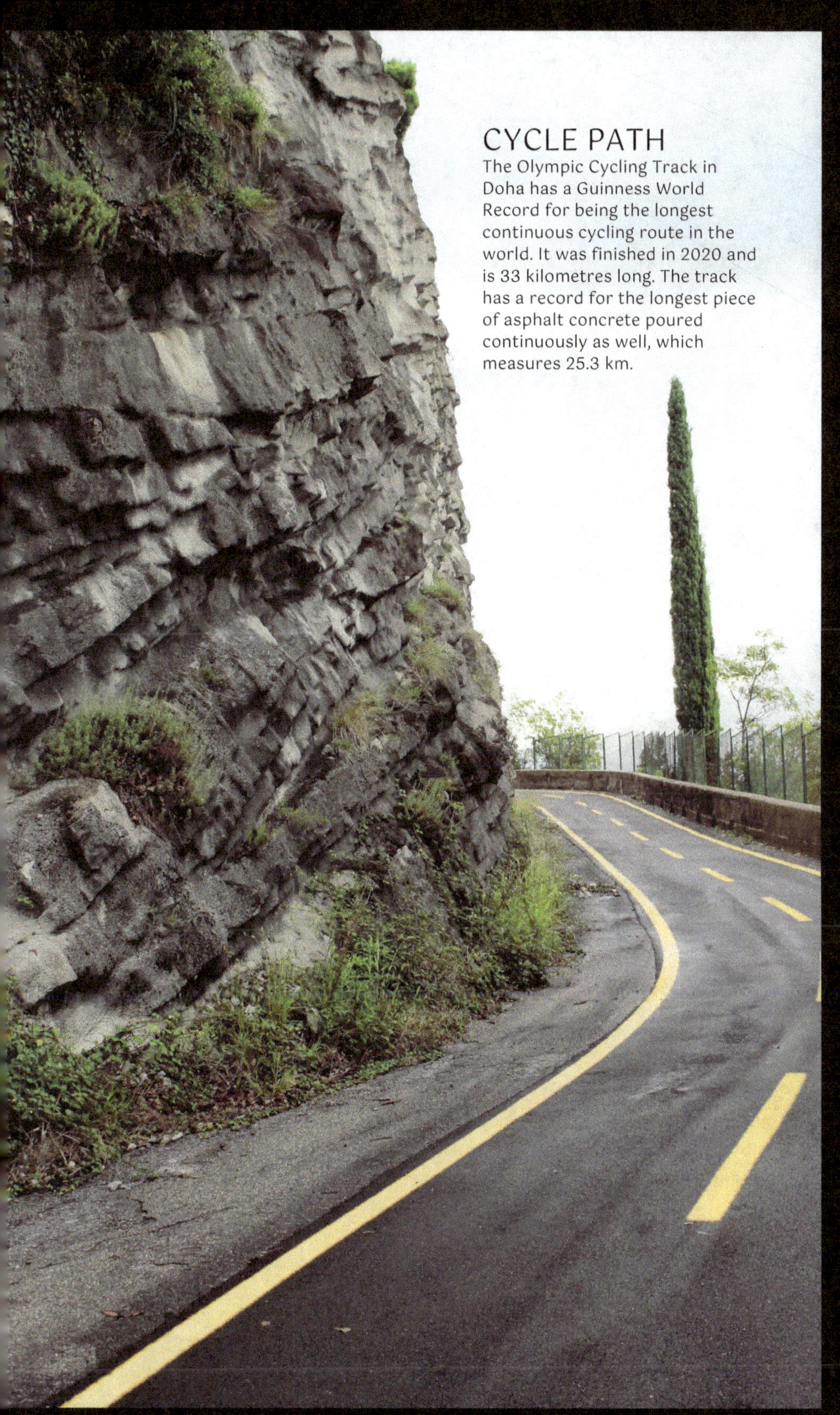

CYCLE PATH

The Olympic Cycling Track in Doha has a Guinness World Record for being the longest continuous cycling route in the world. It was finished in 2020 and is 33 kilometres long. The track has a record for the longest piece of asphalt concrete poured continuously as well, which measures 25.3 km.

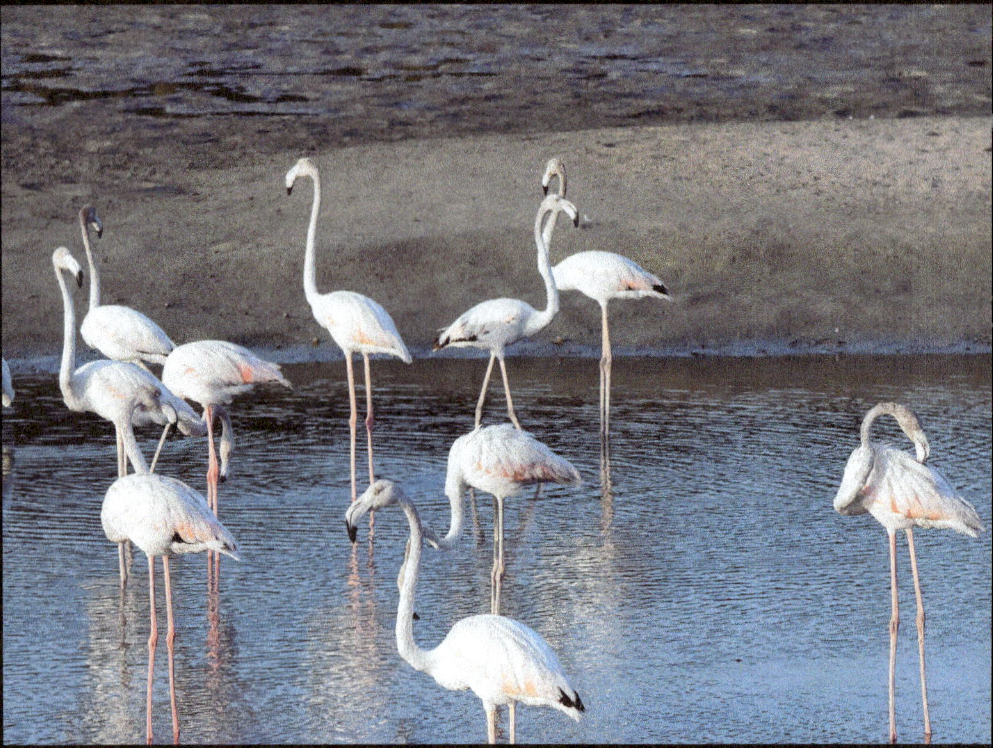

NATURAL RESERVE

Khor Al-Adaid is one of the few places in the world where the sea meets the desert. The area was declared a natural reserve in 2007 and is also known as the Inland Sea. There is a thriving ecology in the area, with some endangered marine species and grazing camels around. Khor Al Adaid has different cultural and archaeological sites to explore as well.

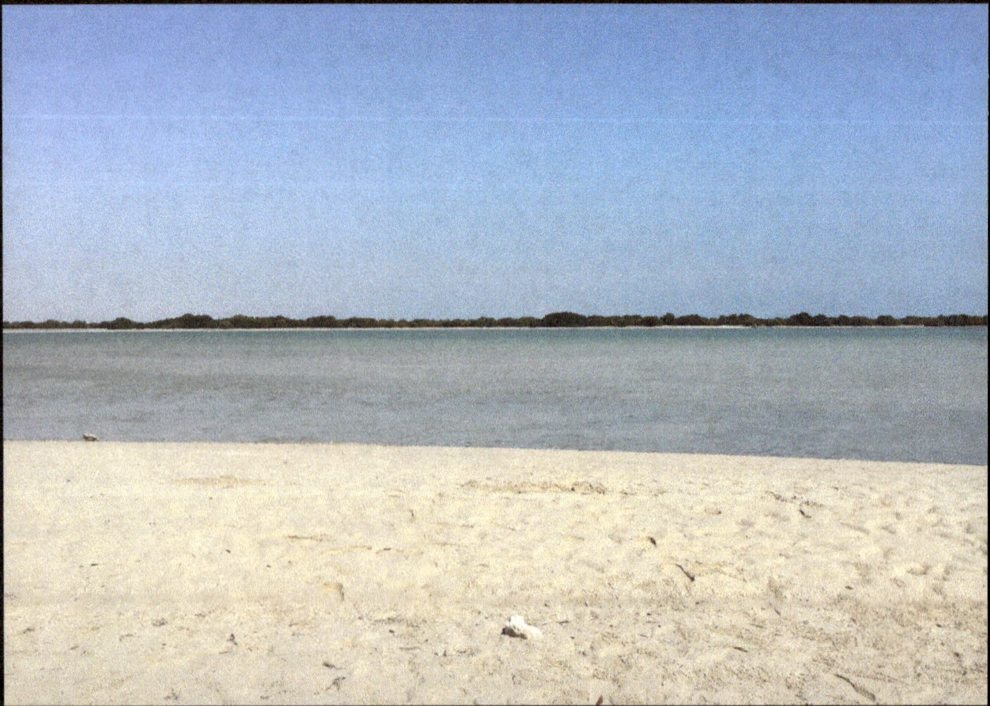

OIL WELL

The oil well is named BD-04-A and has a total length of 40,320 ft MDRT. It is located in the Al-Shaheen offshore oil field off the coast of Qatar. The well also holds a Guinness World Record, cementing its place as the longest in the world.

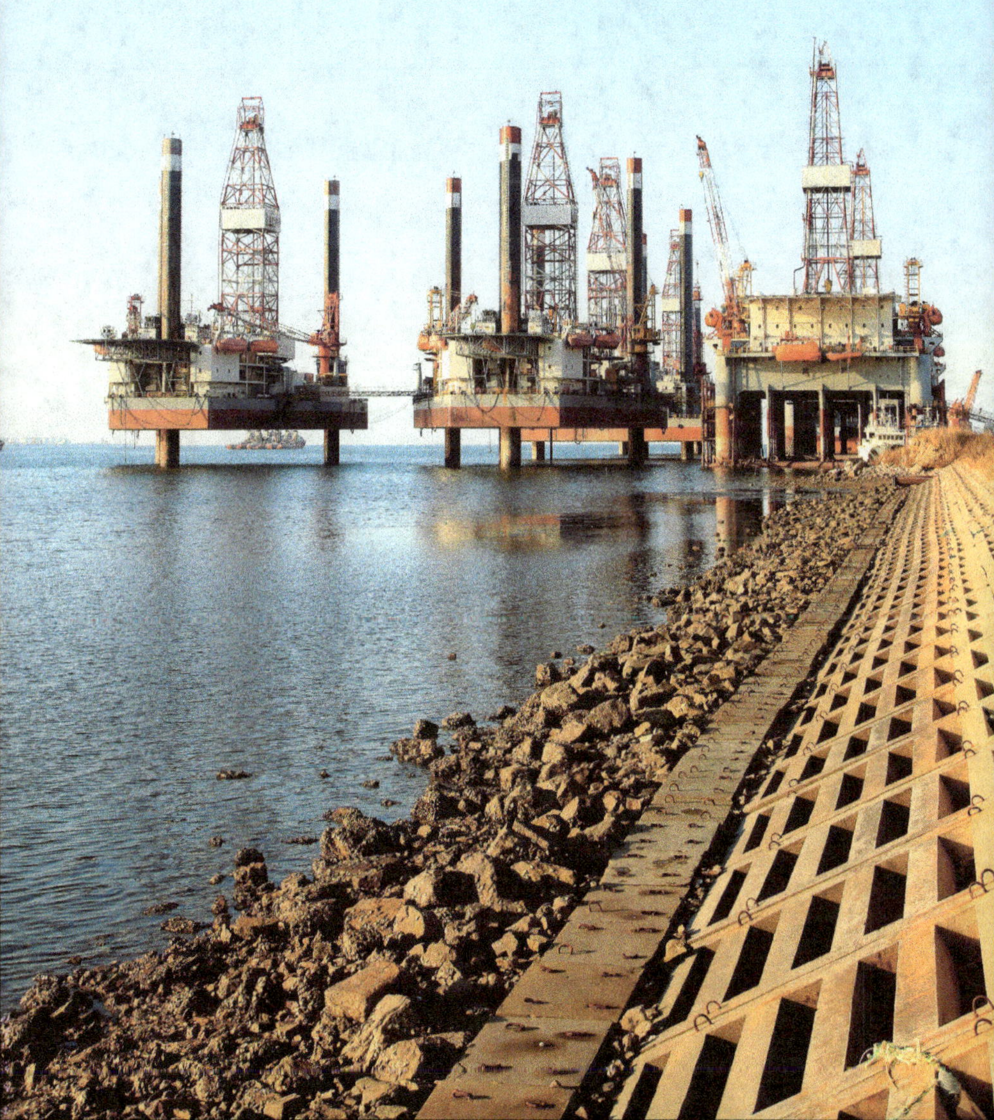

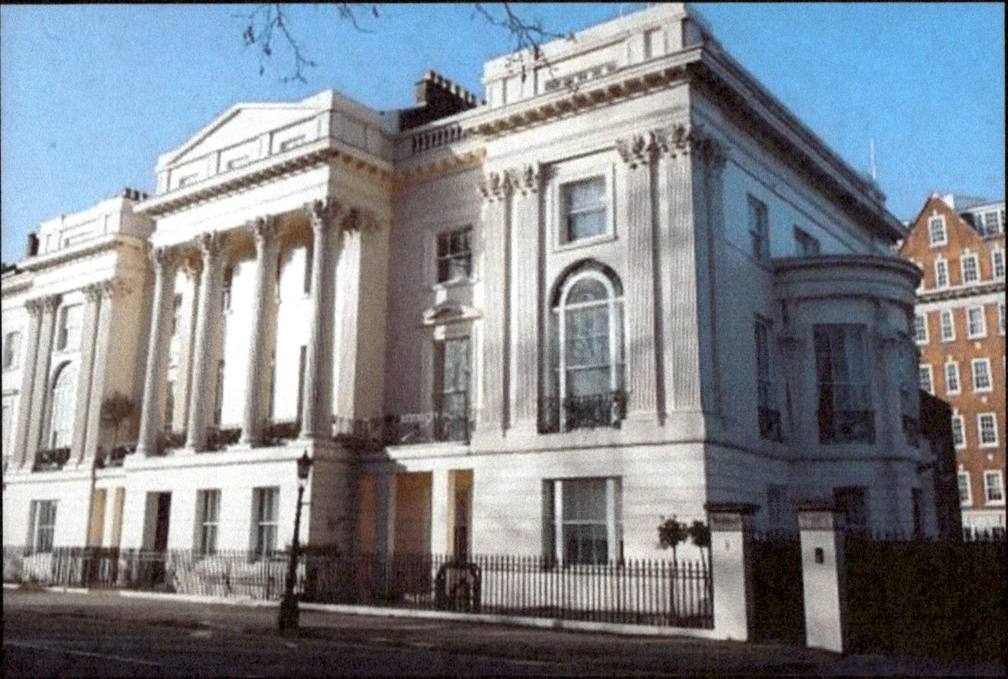

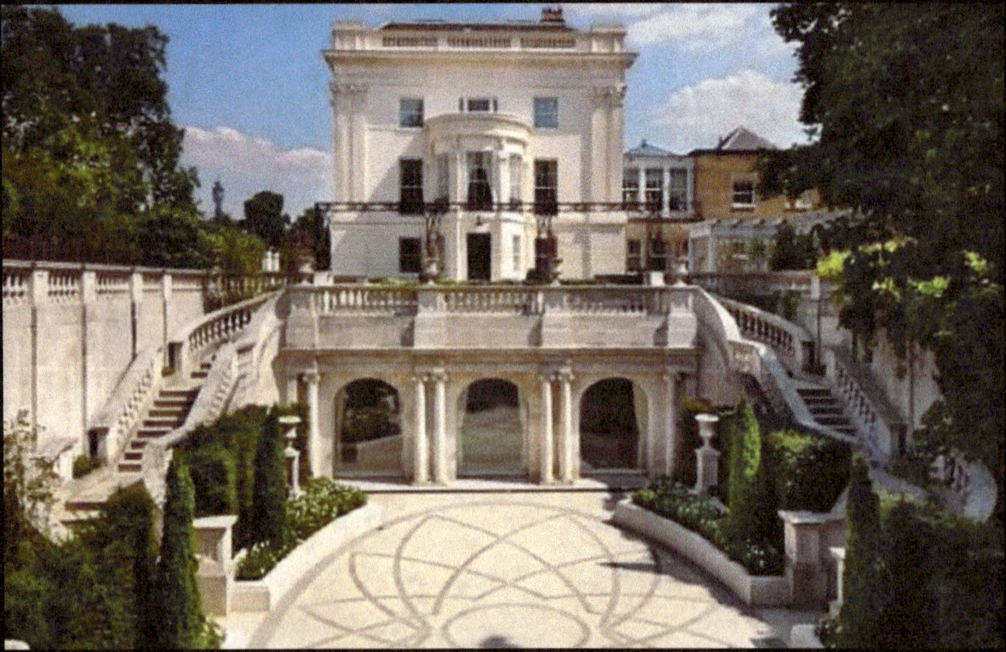

ESTATE

The Qatari Royal Family's new house is being constructed in London for an estimated $313 million. The nation holds more than three times the properties that the Queen owns in London. Qatar is the largest landlord in London, surpassing the Mayor of London and the Queen on this count.

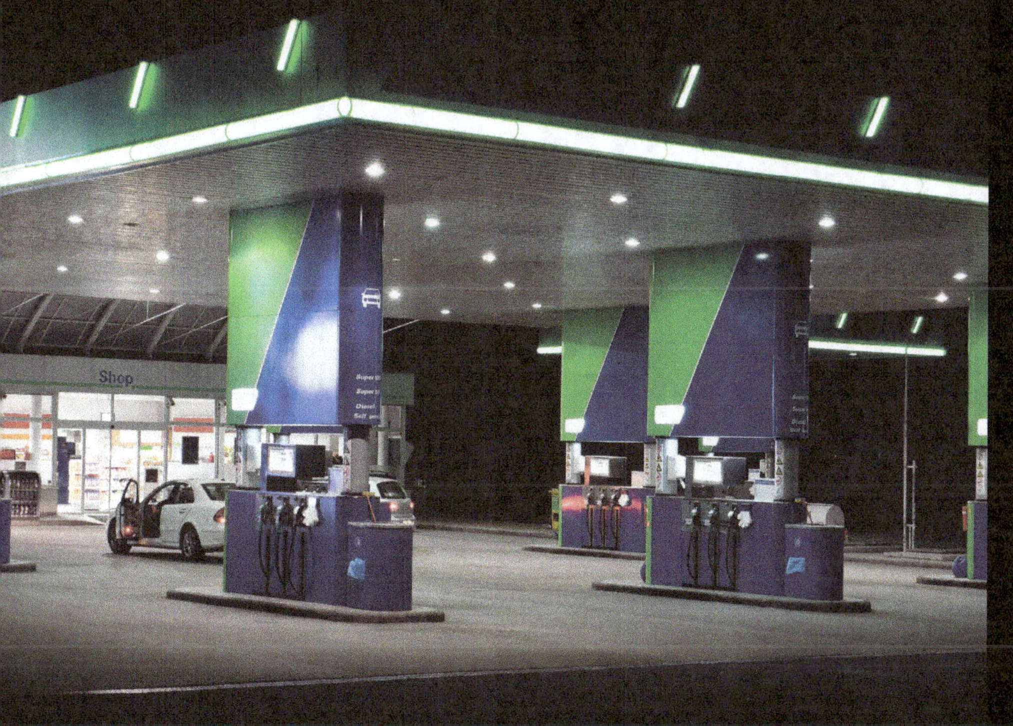

GAS

Qatar is one of the wealthiest countries in the world. Most of their wealth comes from petroleum and natural gas exports. Qataris enjoy very low prices on their petrol and don't have to splash out a lot of cash to fill up their tanks. Filling up your tank in Qatar is cheaper than enjoying a few lattes at Starbucks.

Qatar Travel

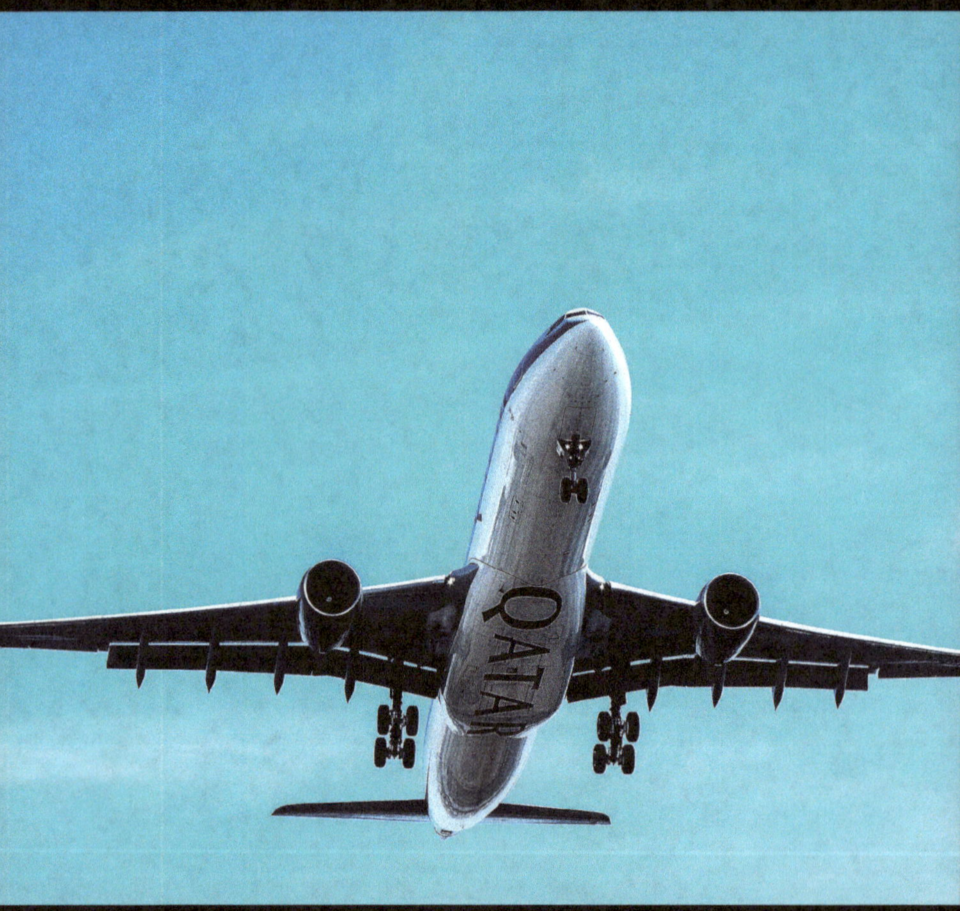

QATAR AIRWAYS

Qatar Airways was chosen the airline of the year at the 2021 Skytrax awards, becoming the only airline ever to take home the prestigious title six times. One of a select few airlines that travels to all seven continents, and at one time, it had the longest regularly scheduled trip in the world between Doha and Auckland, at 16 hours and 30 minutes.

Qatar Airways is the national carrier linking Doha to over 160 international destinations. Plenty of international carriers also fly there; among them are Air India, Asiana Airlines, British Airways, Cathay Pacific, Ethiopian Airlines, Japan Airlines, Philippine Airlines, and Turkish Airlines.

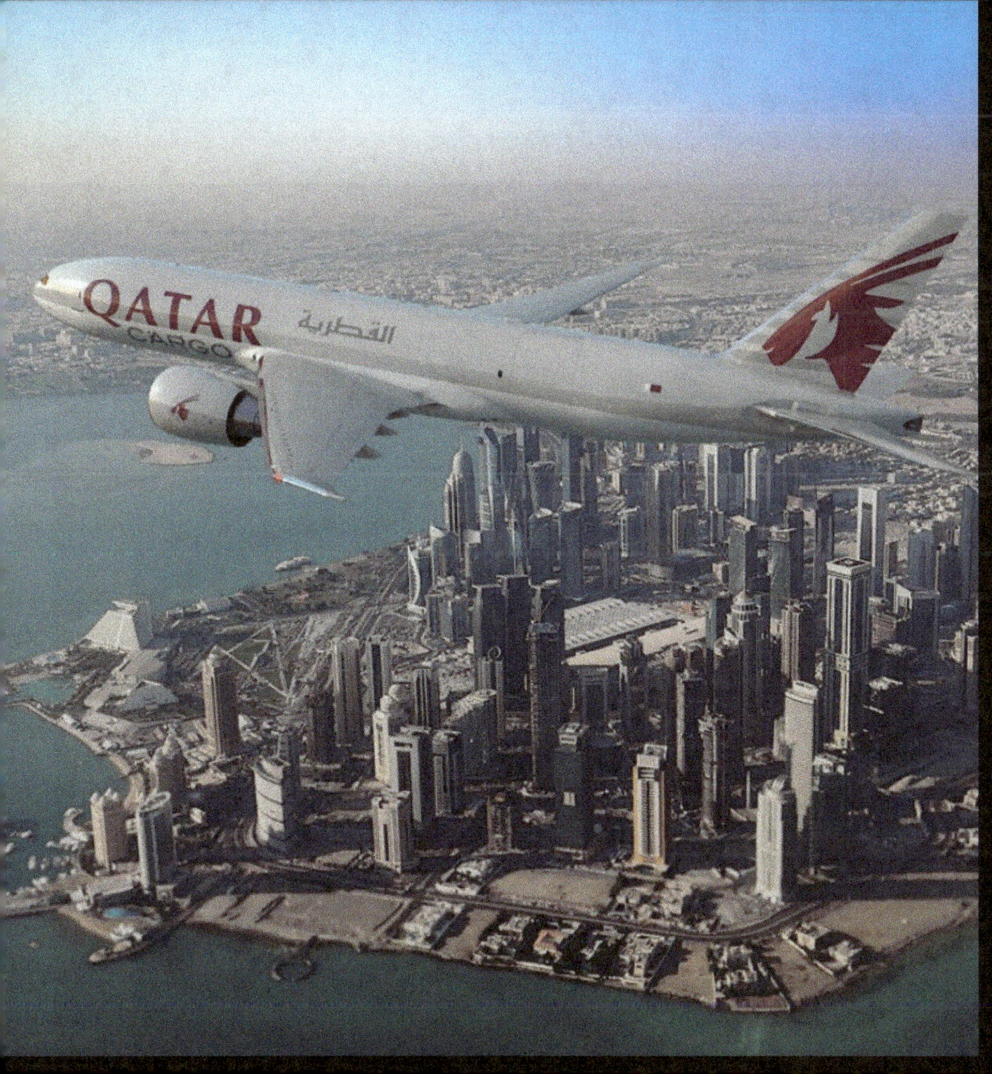

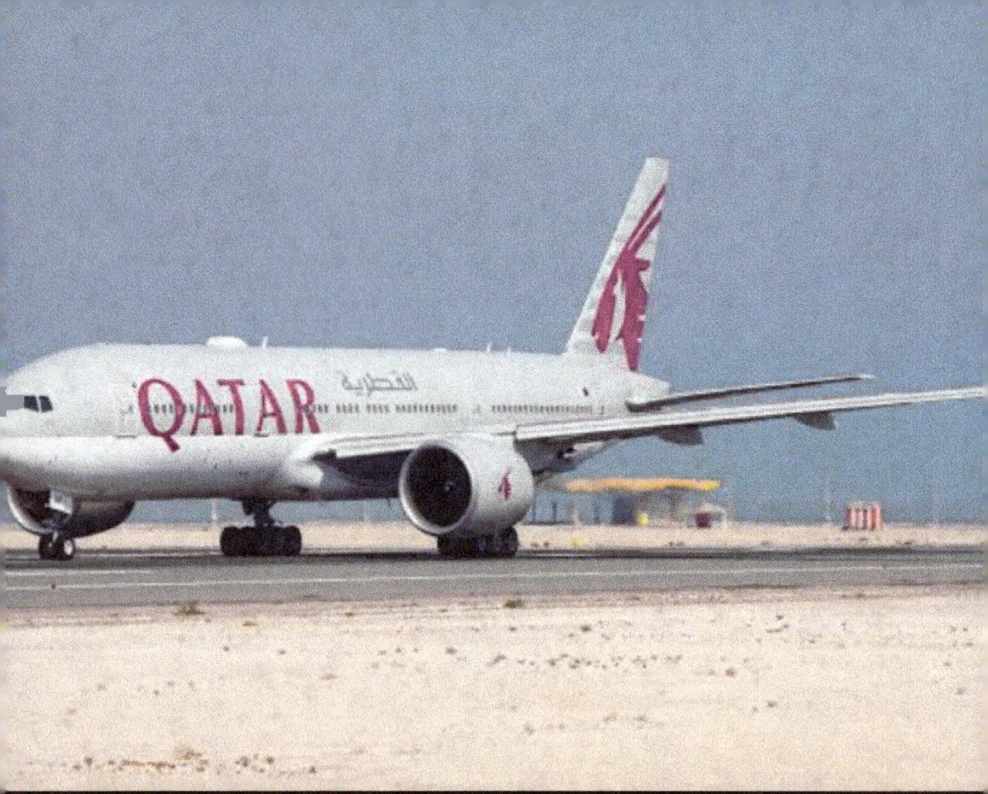

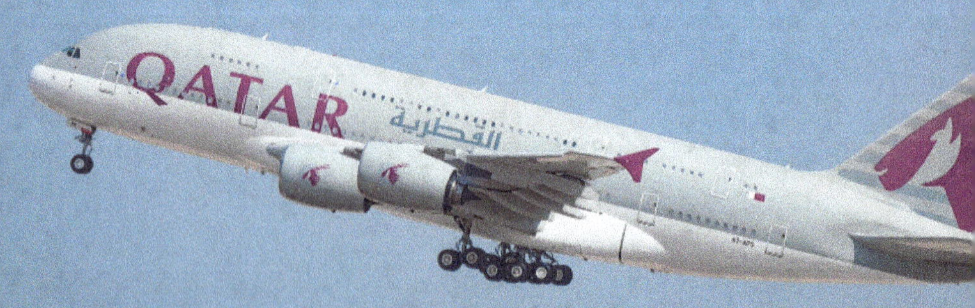

Qatar Airways

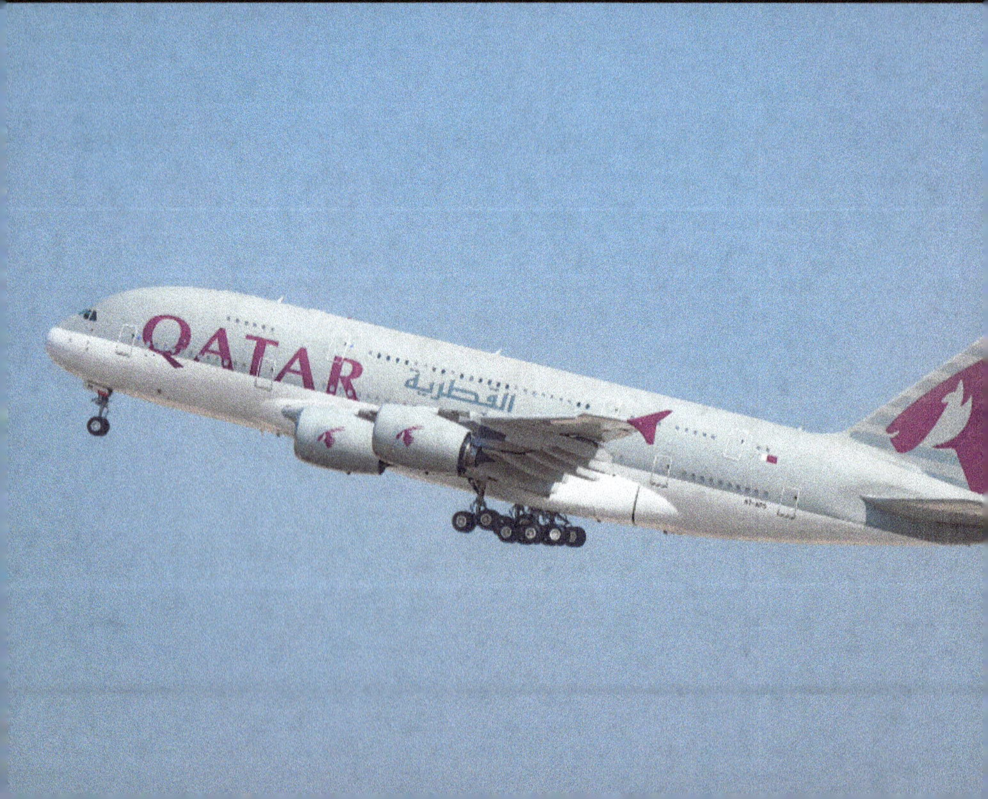

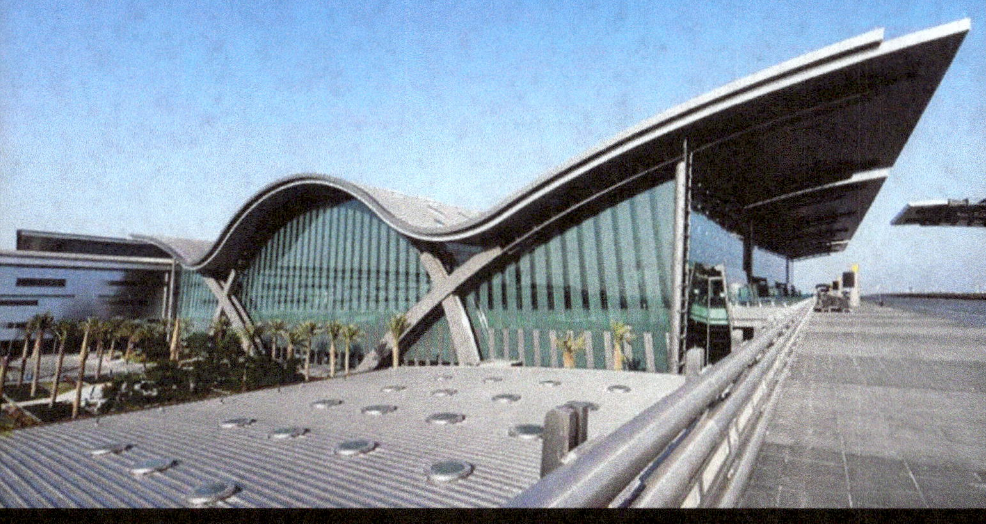

HAMAD INTERNATIONAL AIRPORT

Qatar's Hamad International Airport has been named the best airport in the world by Skytrax World Airport Awards 2021. HIA is home to the longest runway in western Asia, at 15,912 ft, and sixth longest in the world.

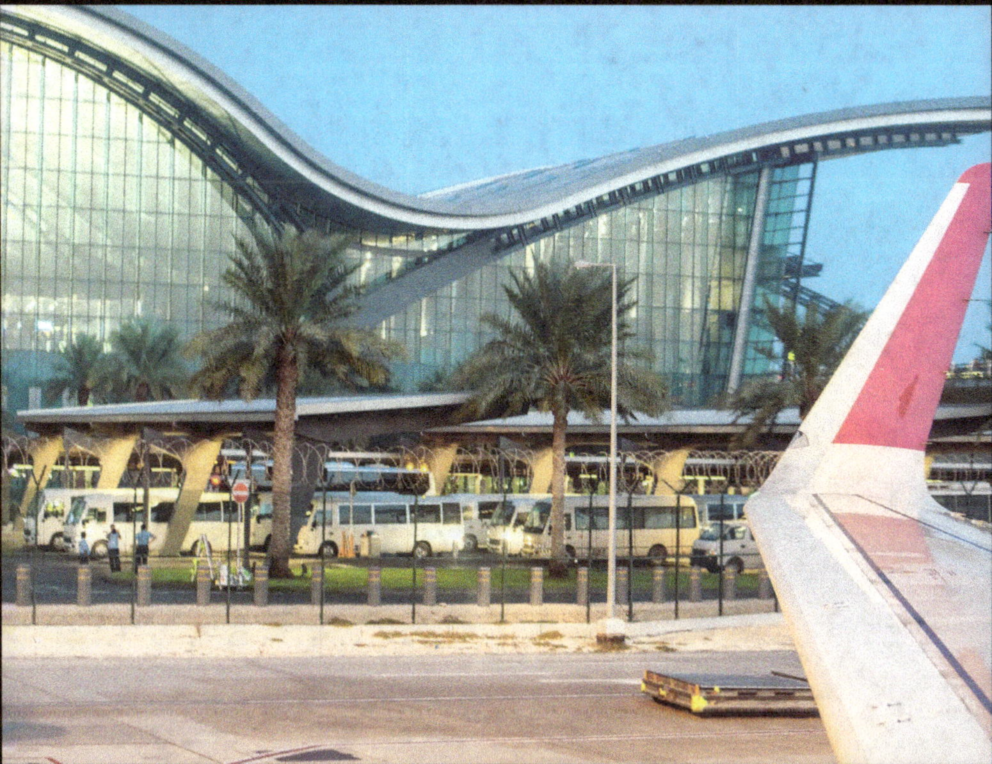

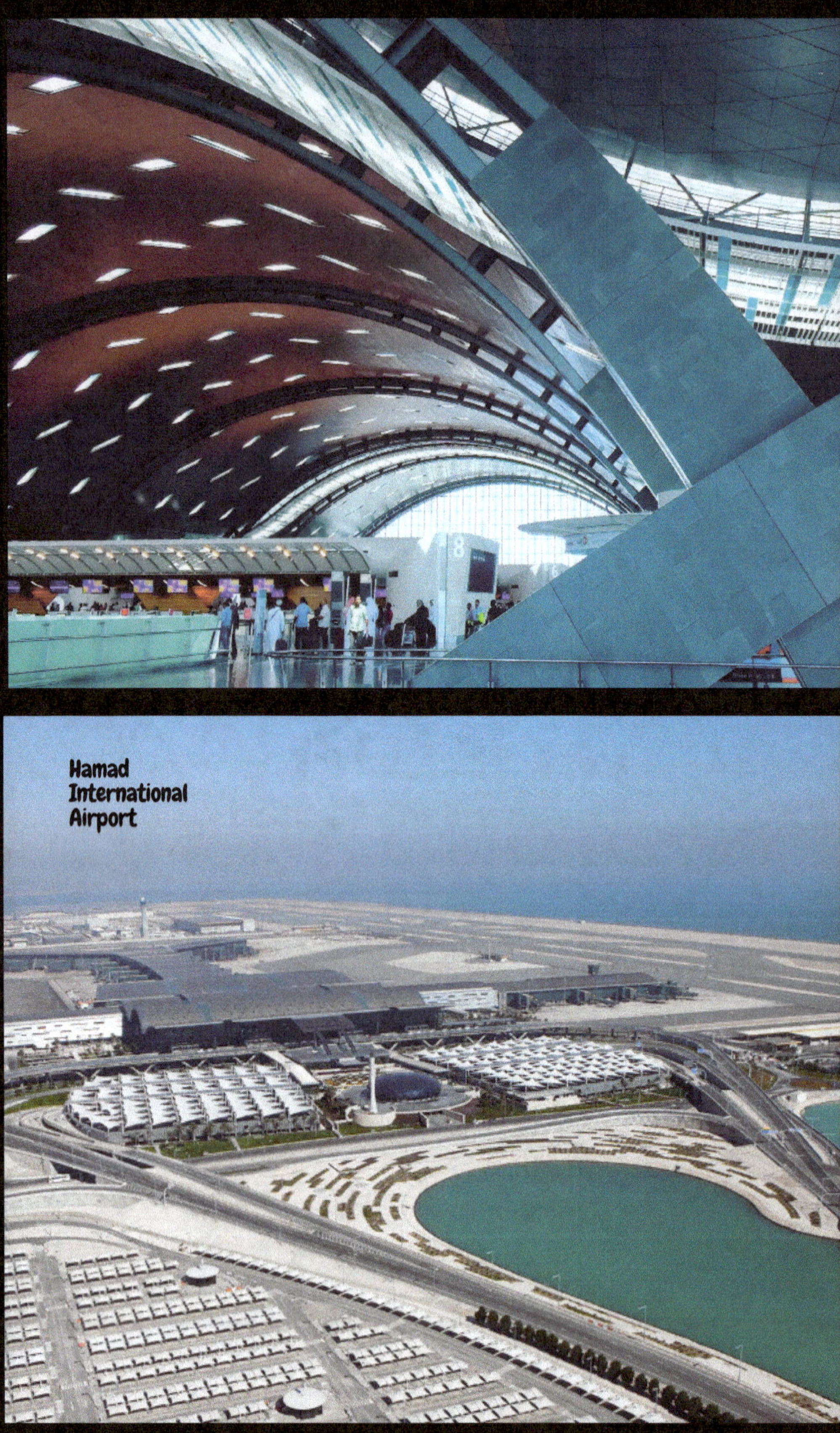
Hamad
International
Airport

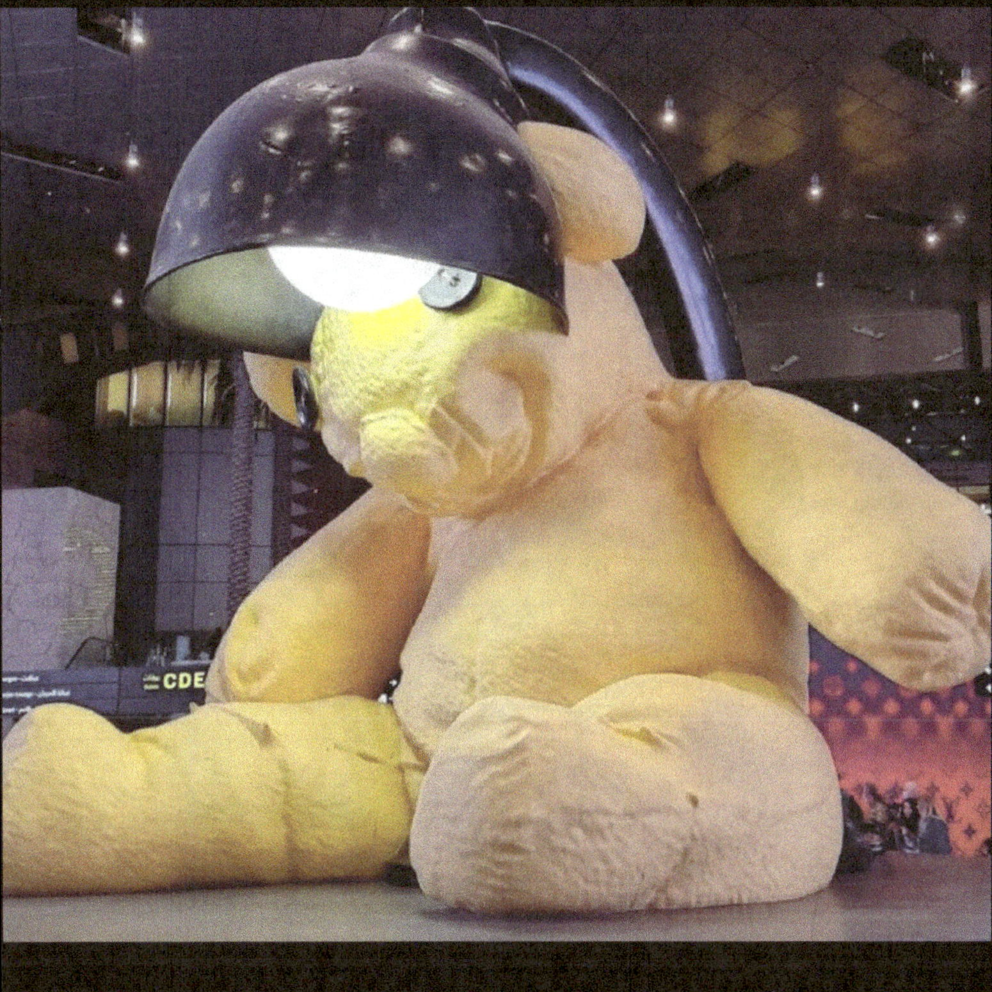

GIANT TEDDY

A giant teddy bear lives at Hamad International Airport. The giant teddy bear has a lamp on its head and sits proudly in the Hamad International Airport. The giant artwork has been reported to cost $6.8 million and weighs almost 20 tonnes. It is sure to catch your eye and has become a very popular picture destination for tourists.

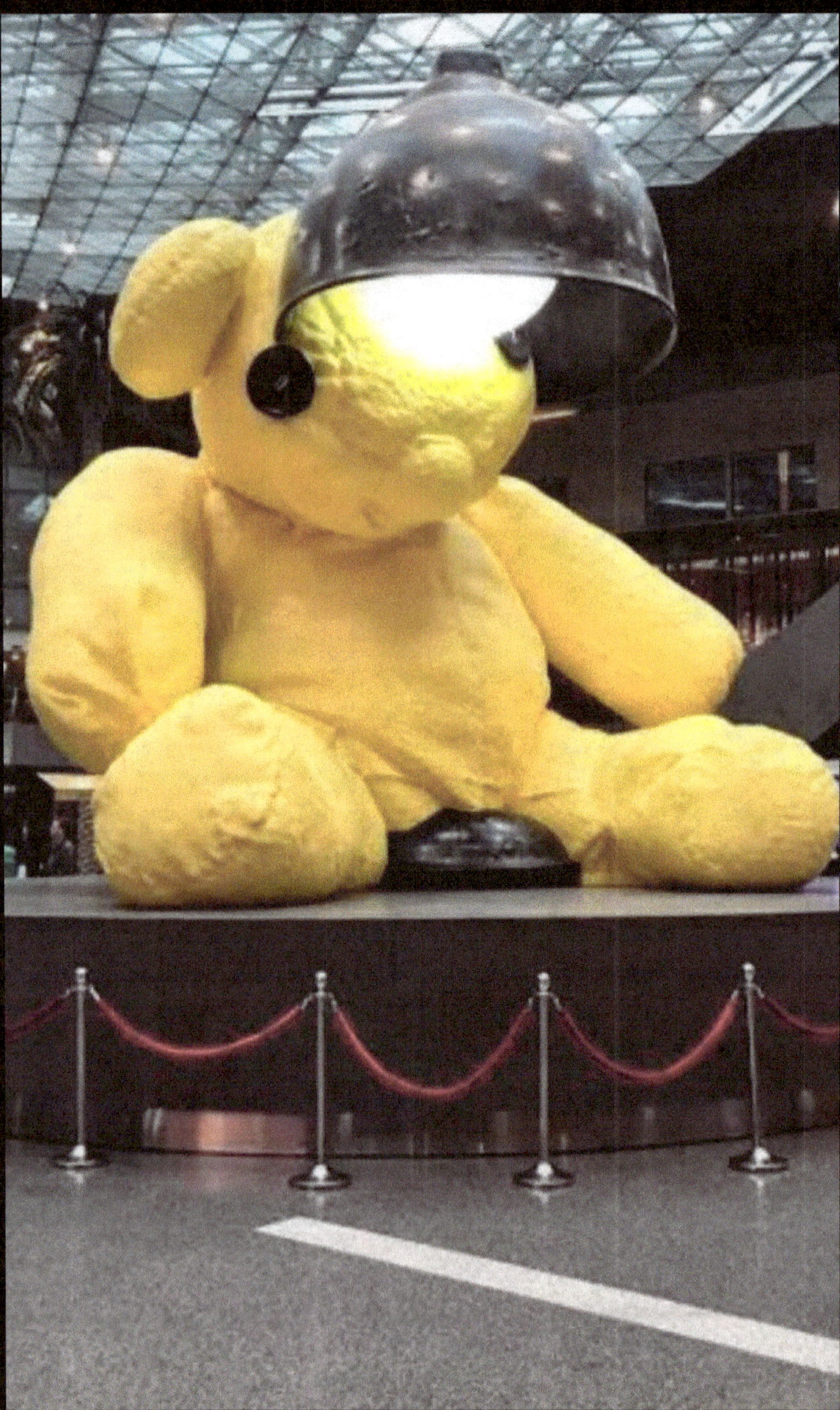

QATAR ANIMALS

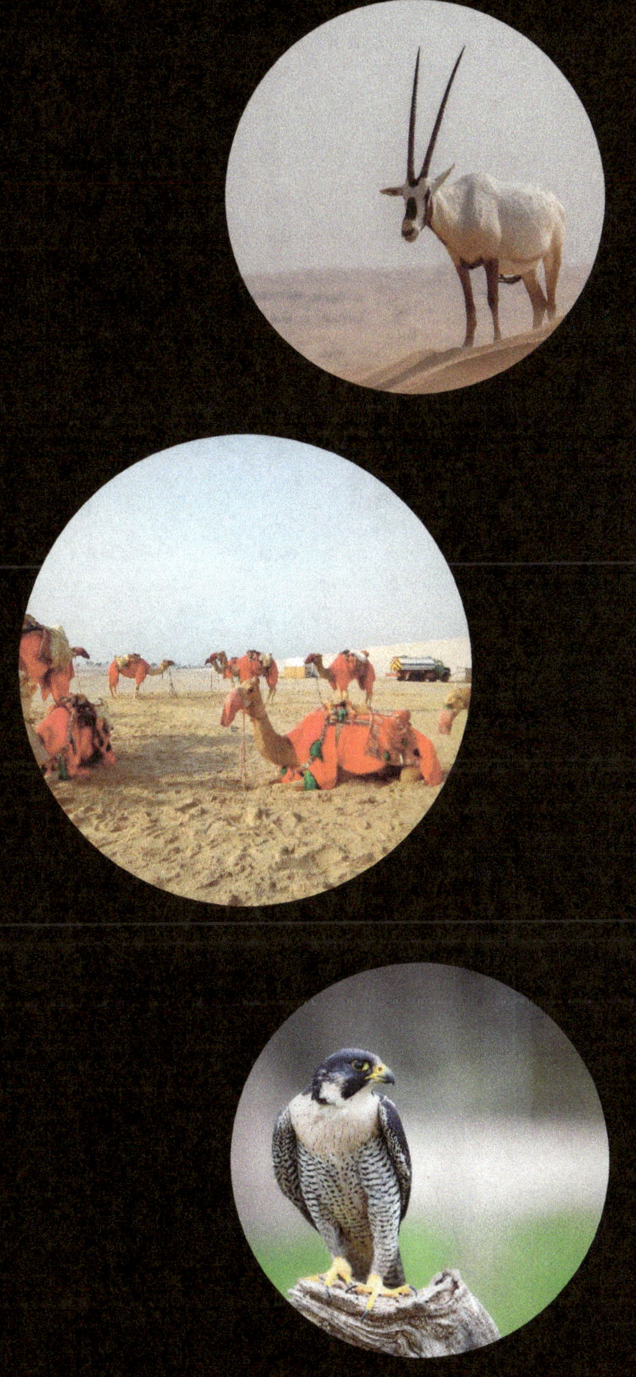

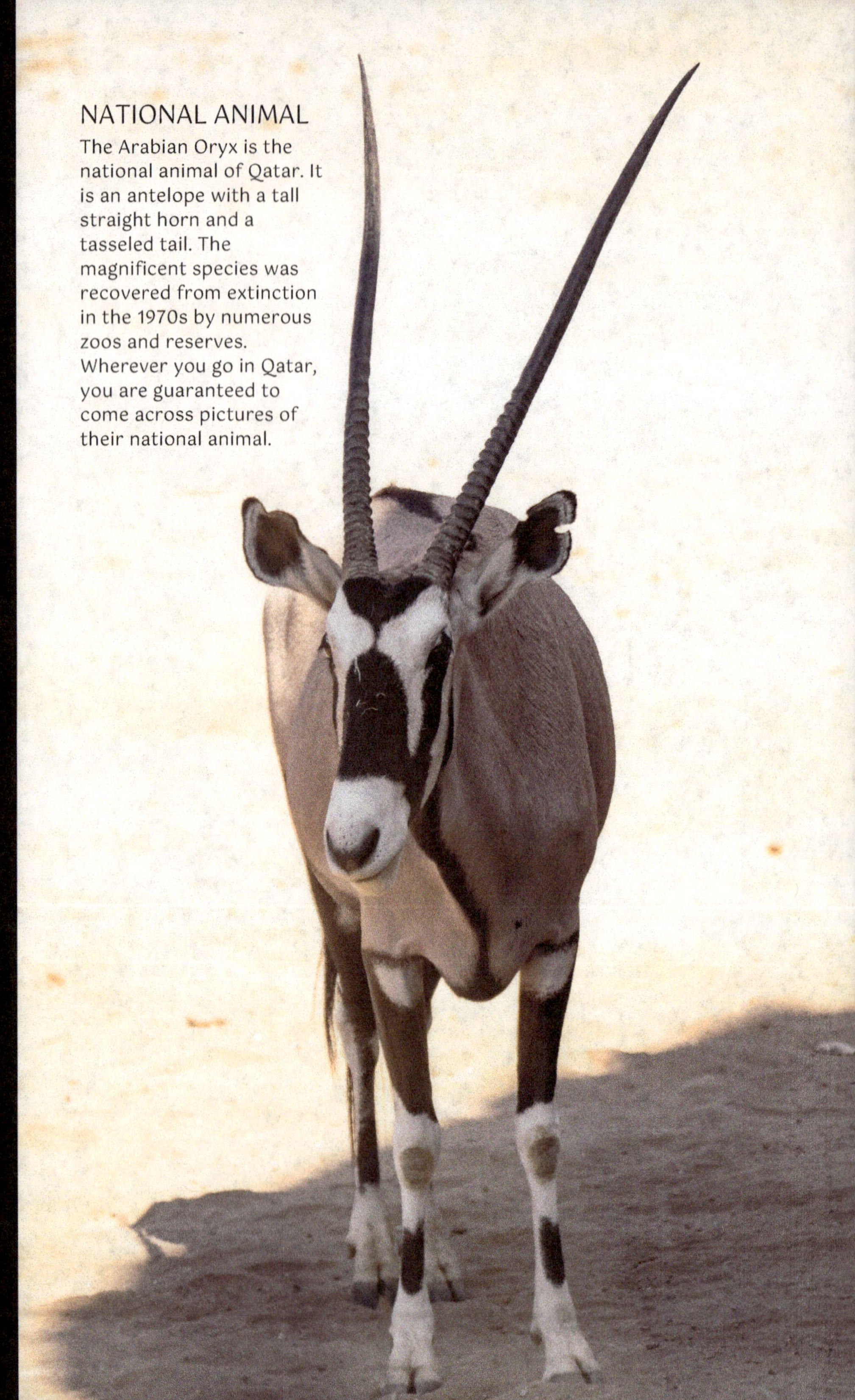

NATIONAL ANIMAL
The Arabian Oryx is the national animal of Qatar. It is an antelope with a tall straight horn and a tasseled tail. The magnificent species was recovered from extinction in the 1970s by numerous zoos and reserves. Wherever you go in Qatar, you are guaranteed to come across pictures of their national animal.

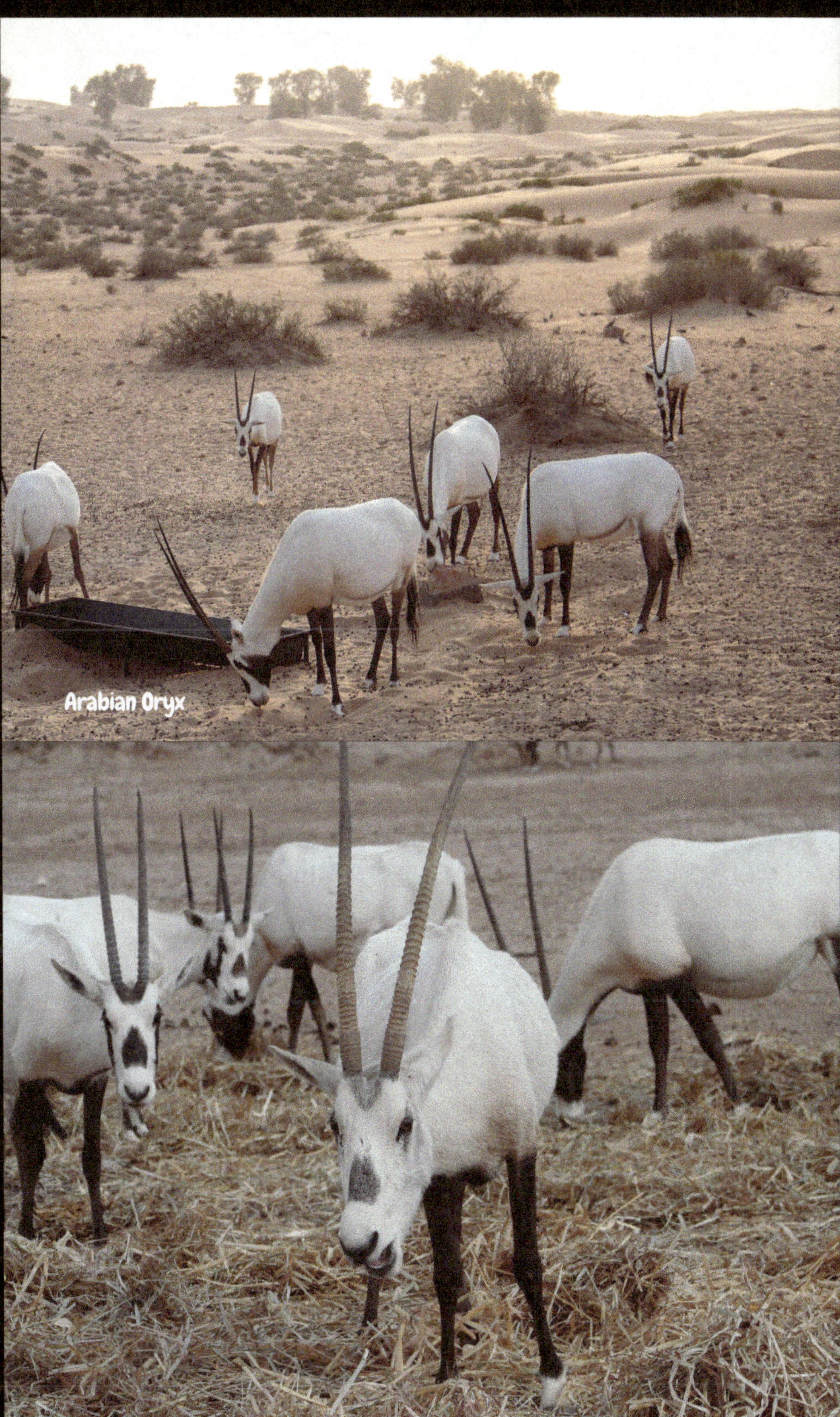
Arabian Oryx

ROBOT

A sport that is hugely popular in Qatar is camel racing, and they use robots to act as jockeys for the races. In the past, children were used, but after it was deemed too dangerous for kids, robots were brought in to take their place. They are controlled by the camel herders remotely, and often these herders will drive alongside the track to have two different perspectives of the race. Camels can run up to 40mph robot jockeys are mounted on them as they race to the finish line

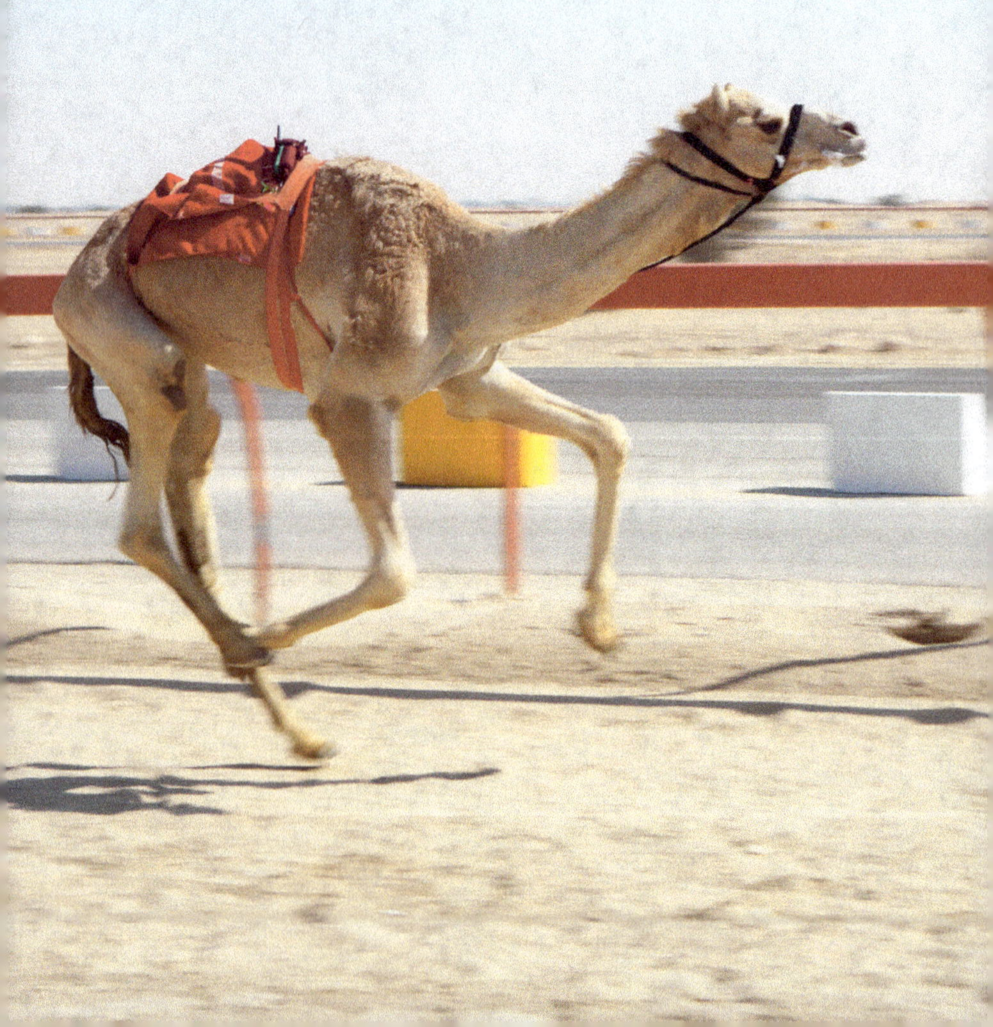

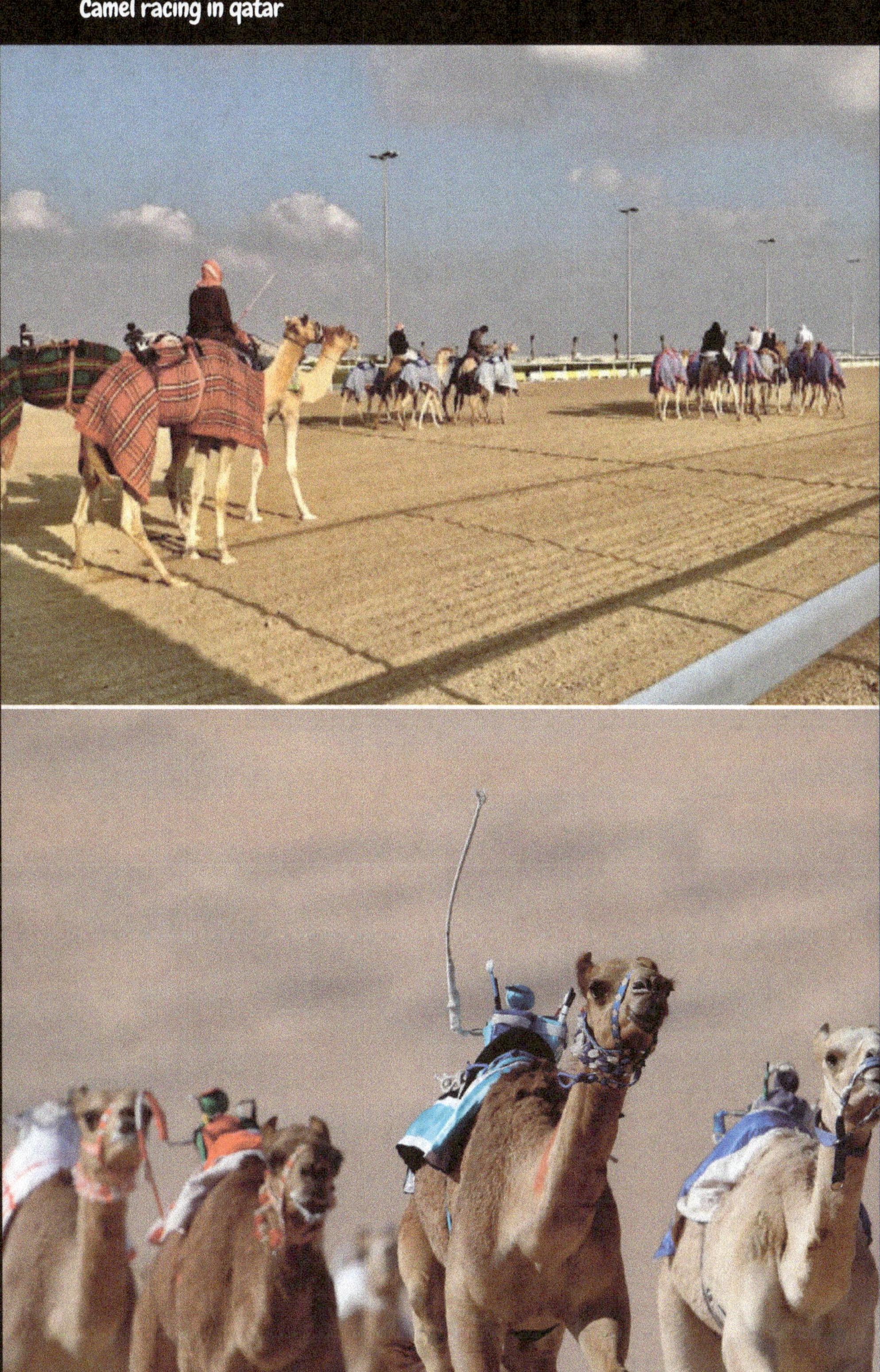

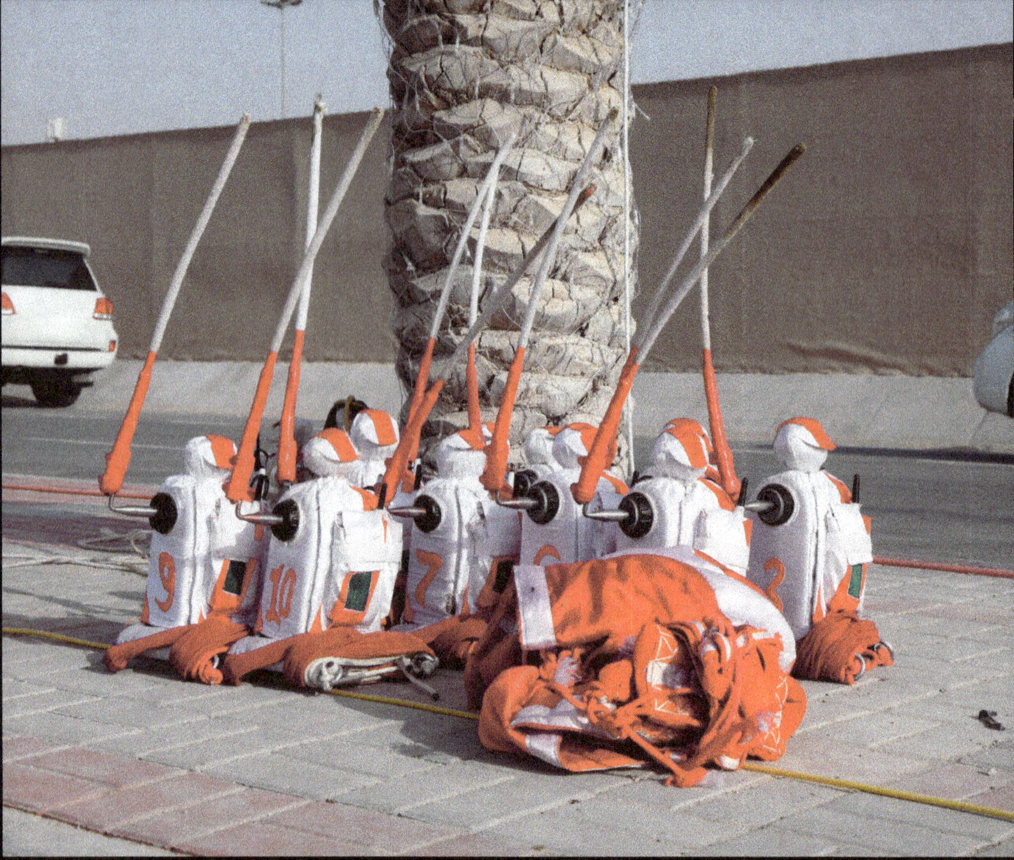

Jockey robots

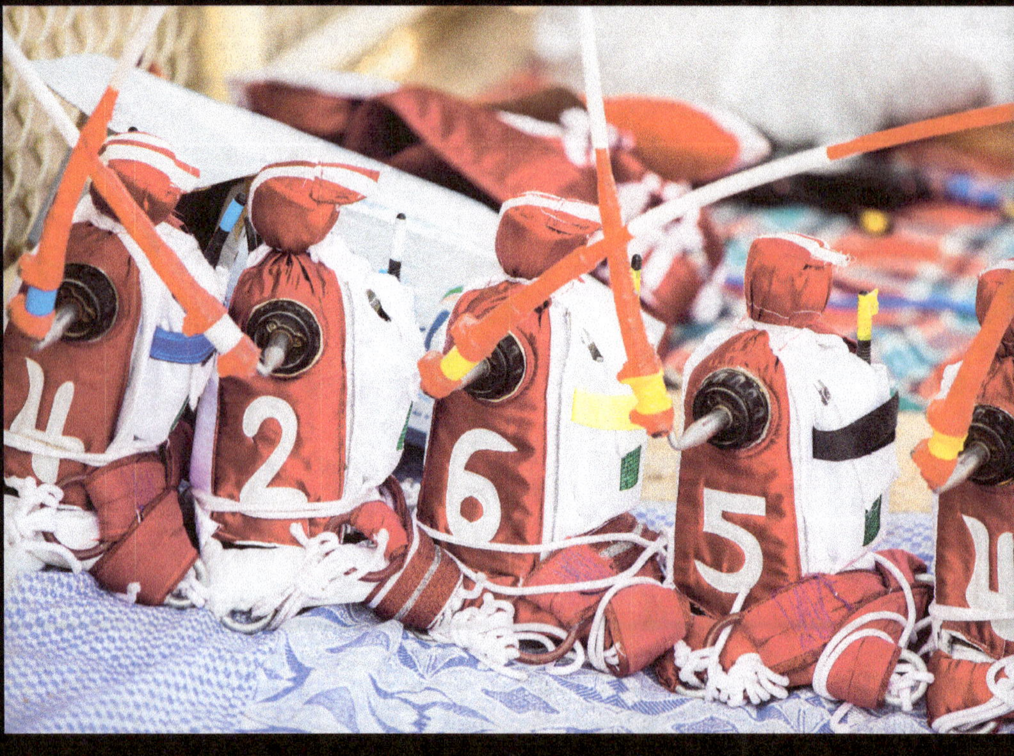

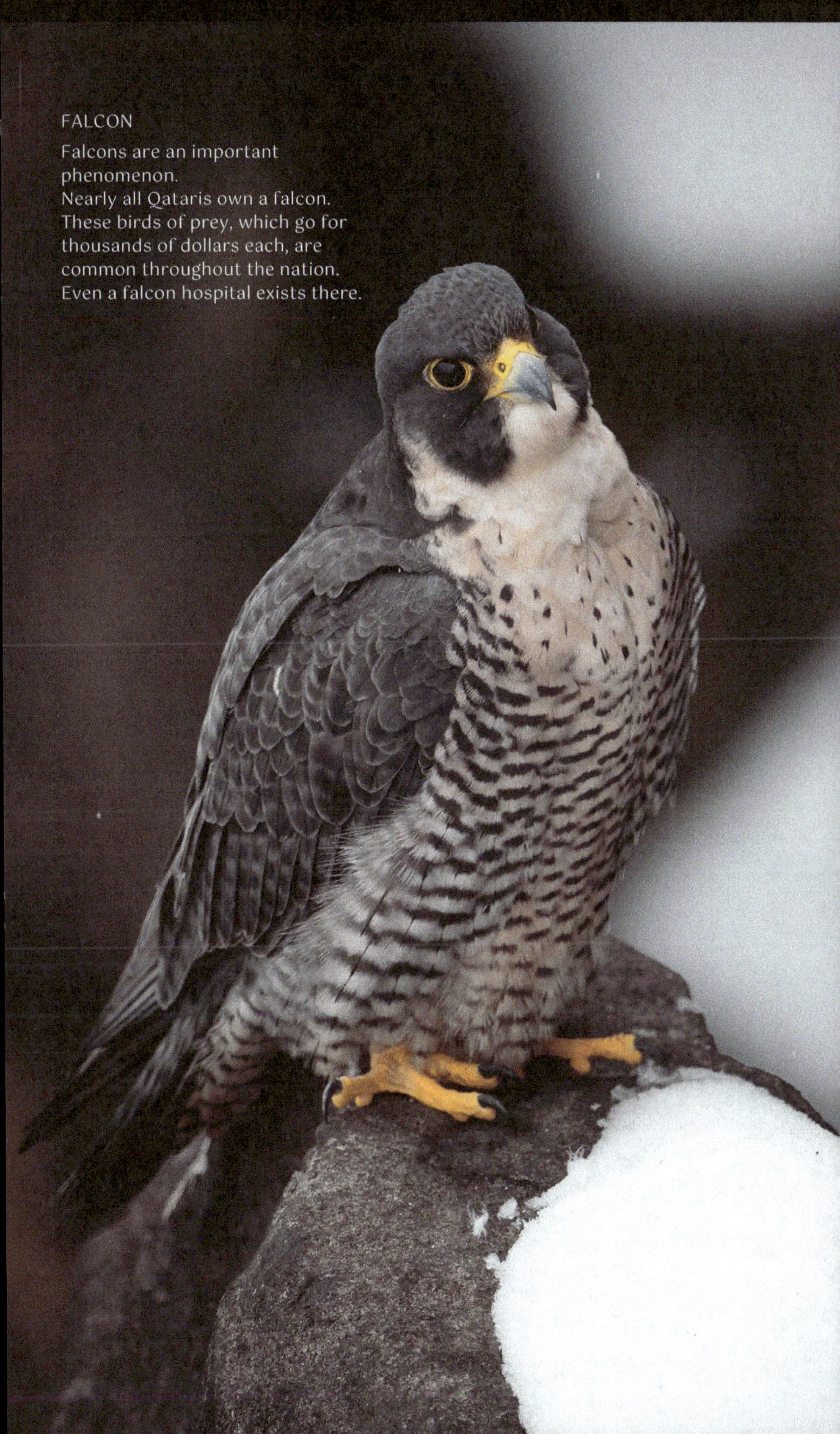

FALCON
Falcons are an important
phenomenon.
Nearly all Qataris own a falcon.
These birds of prey, which go for
thousands of dollars each, are
common throughout the nation.
Even a falcon hospital exists there.

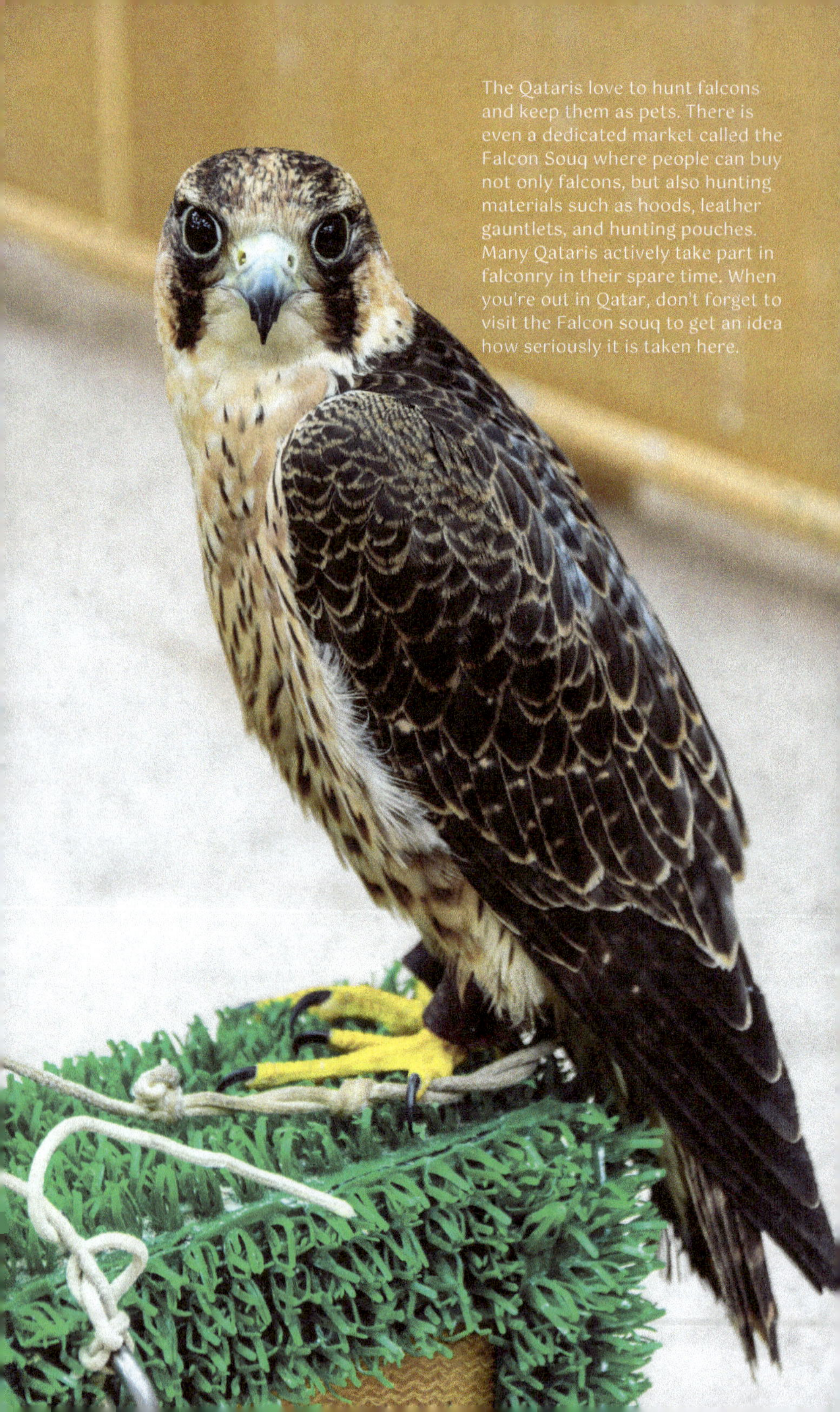

The Qataris love to hunt falcons and keep them as pets. There is even a dedicated market called the Falcon Souq where people can buy not only falcons, but also hunting materials such as hoods, leather gauntlets, and hunting pouches. Many Qataris actively take part in falconry in their spare time. When you're out in Qatar, don't forget to visit the Falcon souq to get an idea how seriously it is taken here.

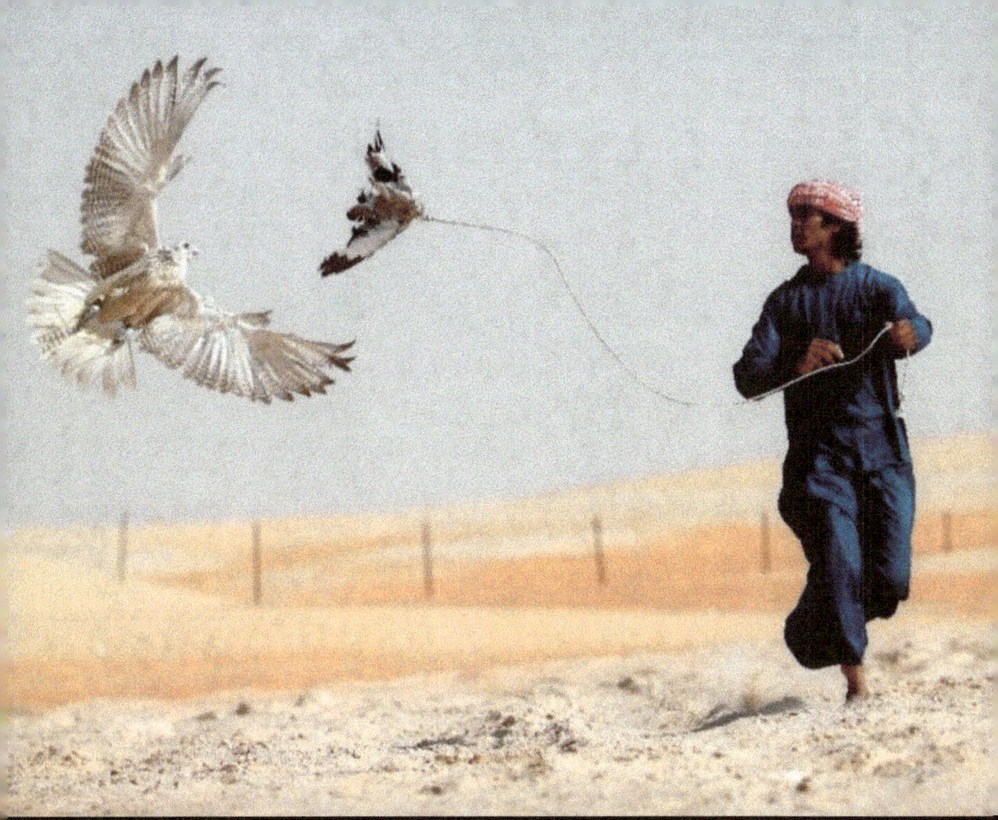

Falconry in qatar

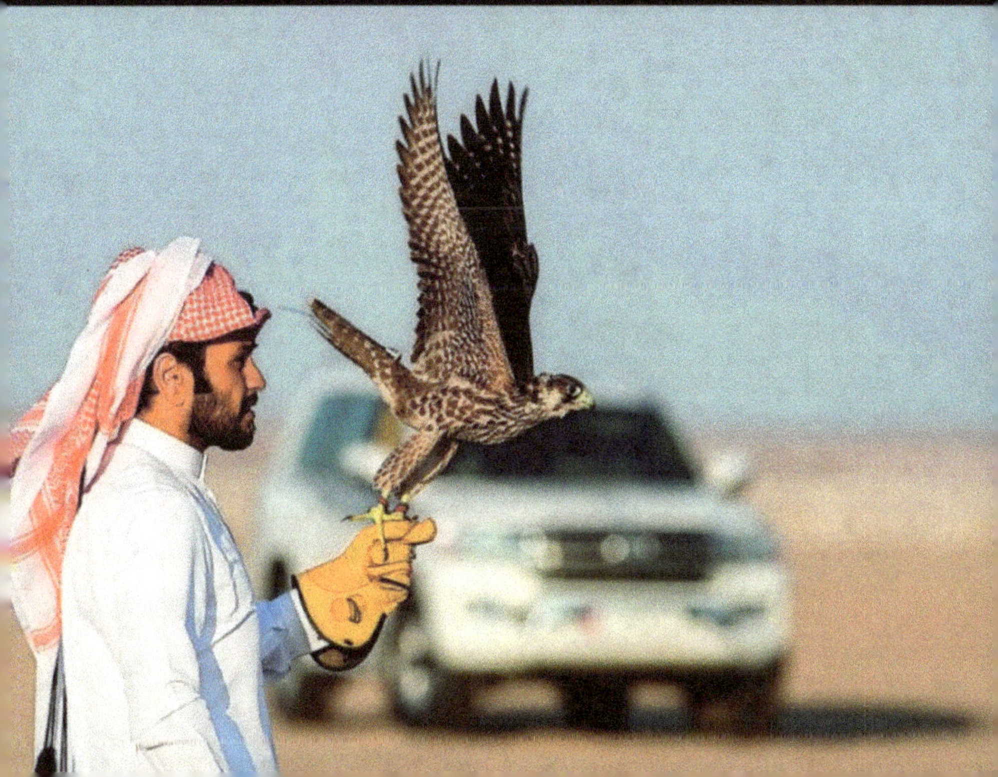

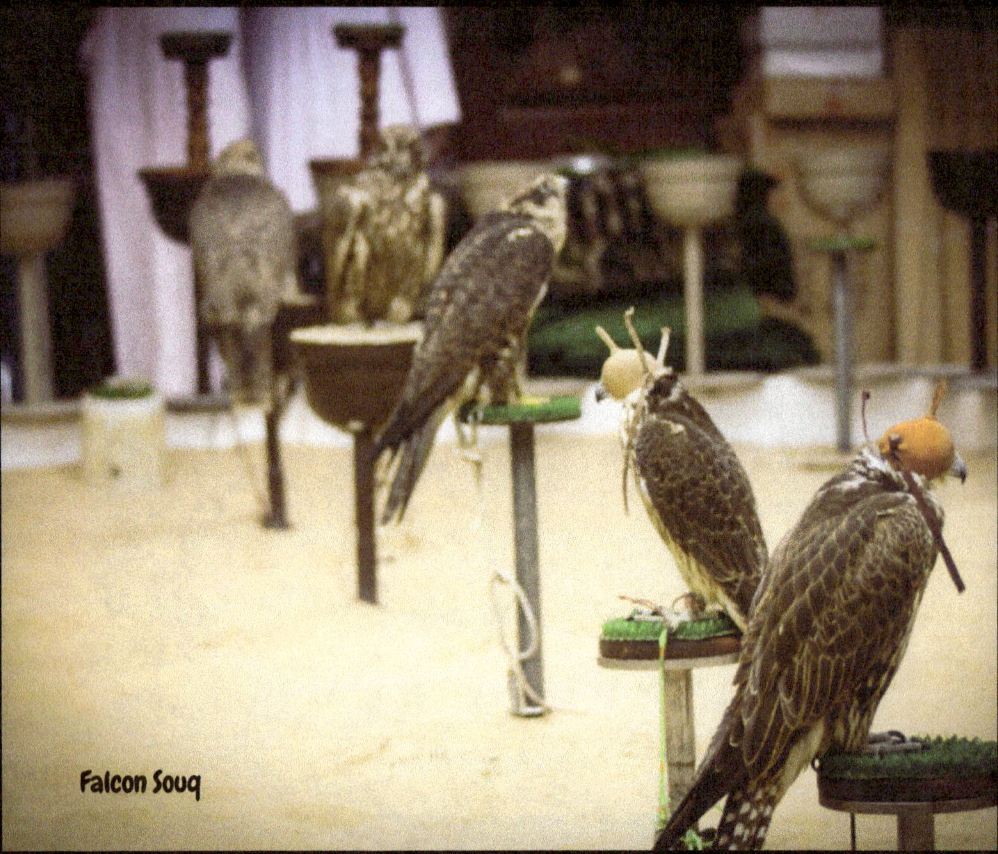

Falcon Souq

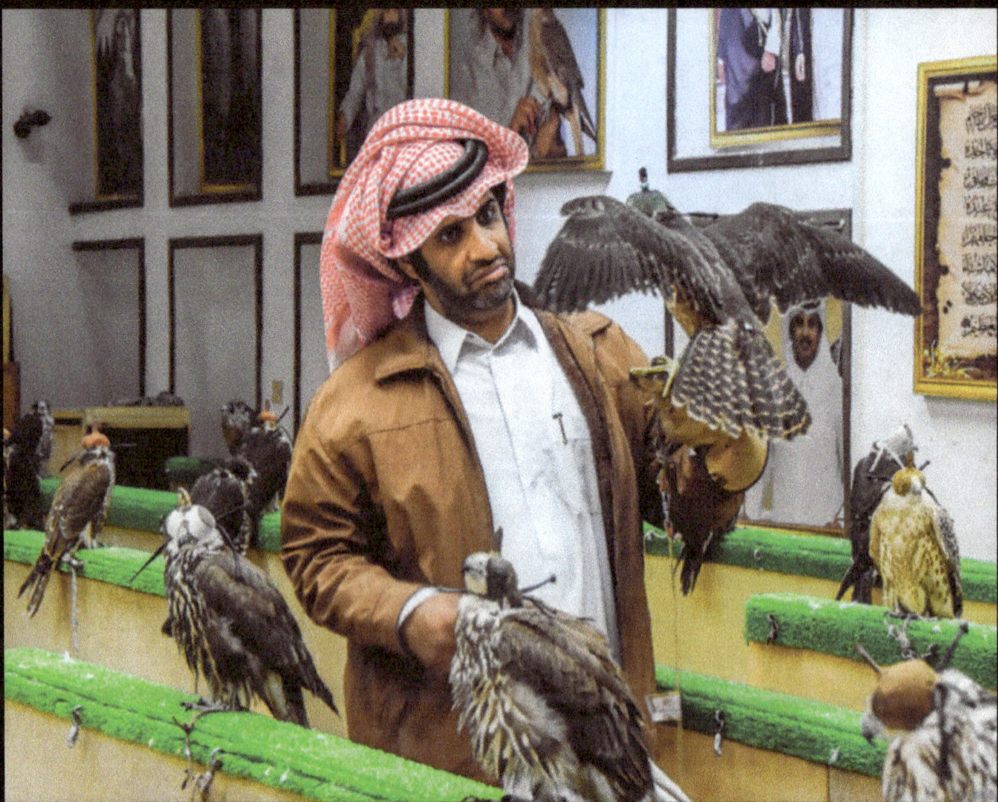

- ## SAFE COUNTRY

Qatar is the second safest country in the world, according to the latest Numbeo crime index. It has the second lowest crime rate, with 14.03 points out of 100, just after Abu Dhabi at 11.72. This isn't the first time Qatar has been listed as one of the safest locations - it was also named the safest city in 2017 and 2019, too.

- ## MEN & WOMEN

Men outnumber women by three to one
According to the latest census numbers from December 2020, males outweigh women in Doha by roughly three to one, with only 811,600 women in a population of 2,846,118. In fact, Qatar has the greatest male to female ratio in the world, with the global average male/female ratio being at 1.02. The UAE and Bahrain similarly have high male/female ratios, with 2.56 and 1.53 respectively.

- ## EXPATS

Qatar is obviously an enticing country to expats, who come here for the excellent weather, the easygoing lifestyle and, of course, the tax-free earnings. The attraction of Qatar is so tremendous that there are now more than two million expatriates living in the country, which means that Qataris are in the minority, at roughly 15 percent of the population, according to Visit Qatar.

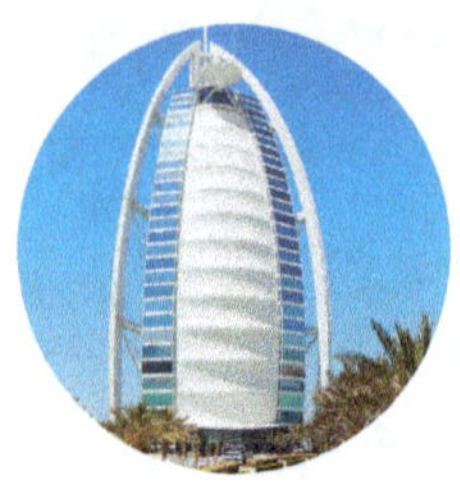

• AL JAZEERA

Al Jazeera was formed in 1996 as part of Qatari aspirations to leverage economic power into political influence in the Arab world and beyond, and continues to receive political and financial support from the government of Qatar. As a consequence, Al Jazeera has been criticized for being Qatari state media.

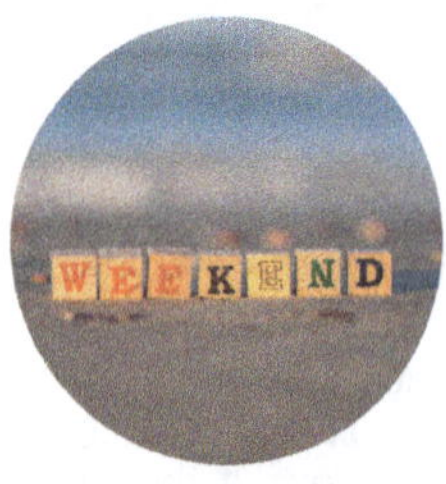

• WEEKENDS

Most of the countries in the UAE don't have the standard weekends that the West knows of. In Islam, Friday is a blessed day, and so many of these countries, including Qatar, don't work on those days. The workweek starts from Sunday and goes up to Thursday.

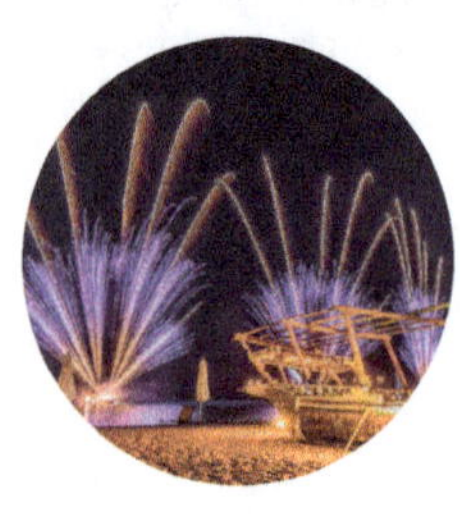

• NATIONAL DAY

Qatar National Day is celebrated every year on December 18 as it marks the day Jassim bin Mohammed Al Thani, who managed to unify the local tribes in Qatar, succeeded his father as ruler back in 1878. Prior to 2007, National Day was actually celebrated on September 3 — the anniversary of Qatar's independence from the British in 1971.

QATAR RANDOM FACTS

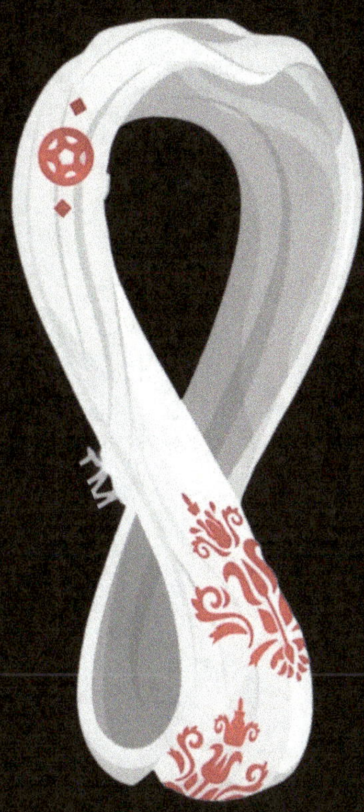

FIFA WORLD CUP
Qatar2022

FIFA WORLD CUP

Qatar will be the first Arab country to host the FIFA World
Cup in 2022. It will also be the smallest nation ever to host it
and the only one to hold it in winter. Furthermore, it will be a
carbon neutral World Cup. Qatar has committed much in
this event, and it promises to be amazing when it comes.

NATIONAL DISH

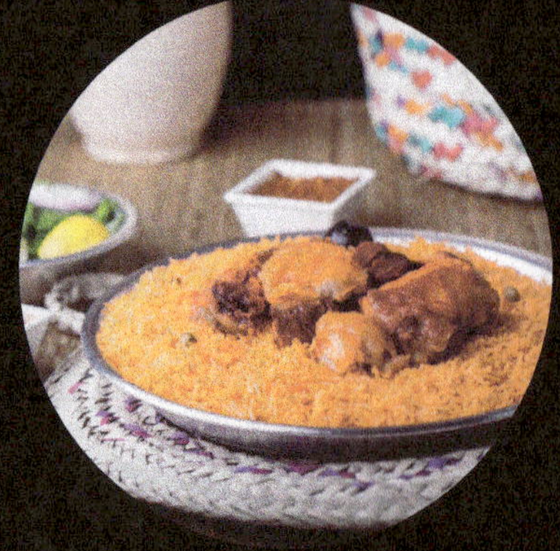

Machboos is the national dish of Qatar and is incredibly popular amongst both locals and tourists.

The dish is made of rice, meat, onions, and tomatoes, mixed with spices, and is sure to leave you wanting more. When you're in Qatar, it would definitely be a very wise decision to try it.

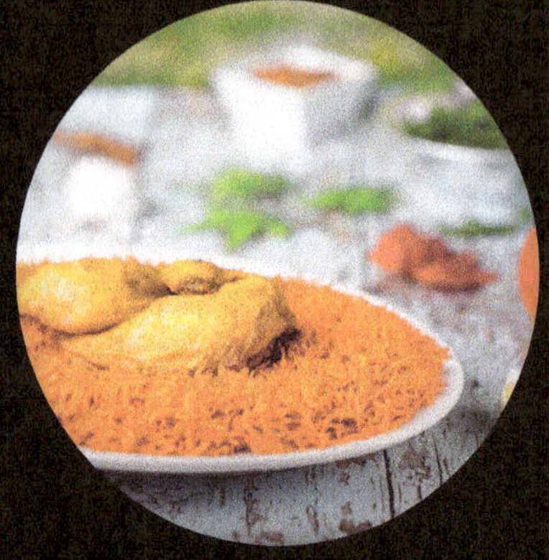

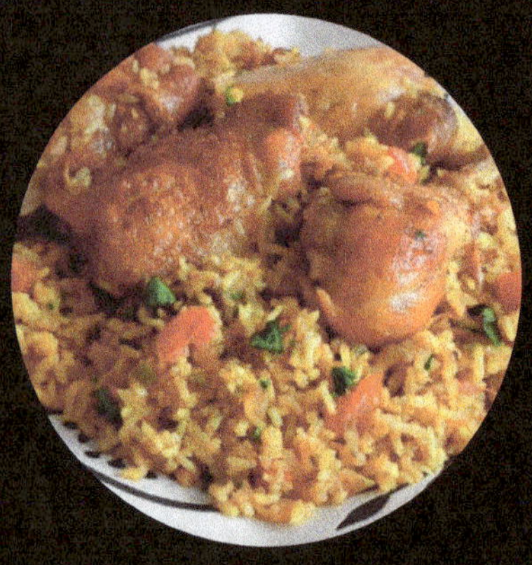

Machboos, also known as Kabsa, made with either lamb or chicken. Machboos or 'kabsa' actually means pressed in Arabic and it has slight variations from region to region.

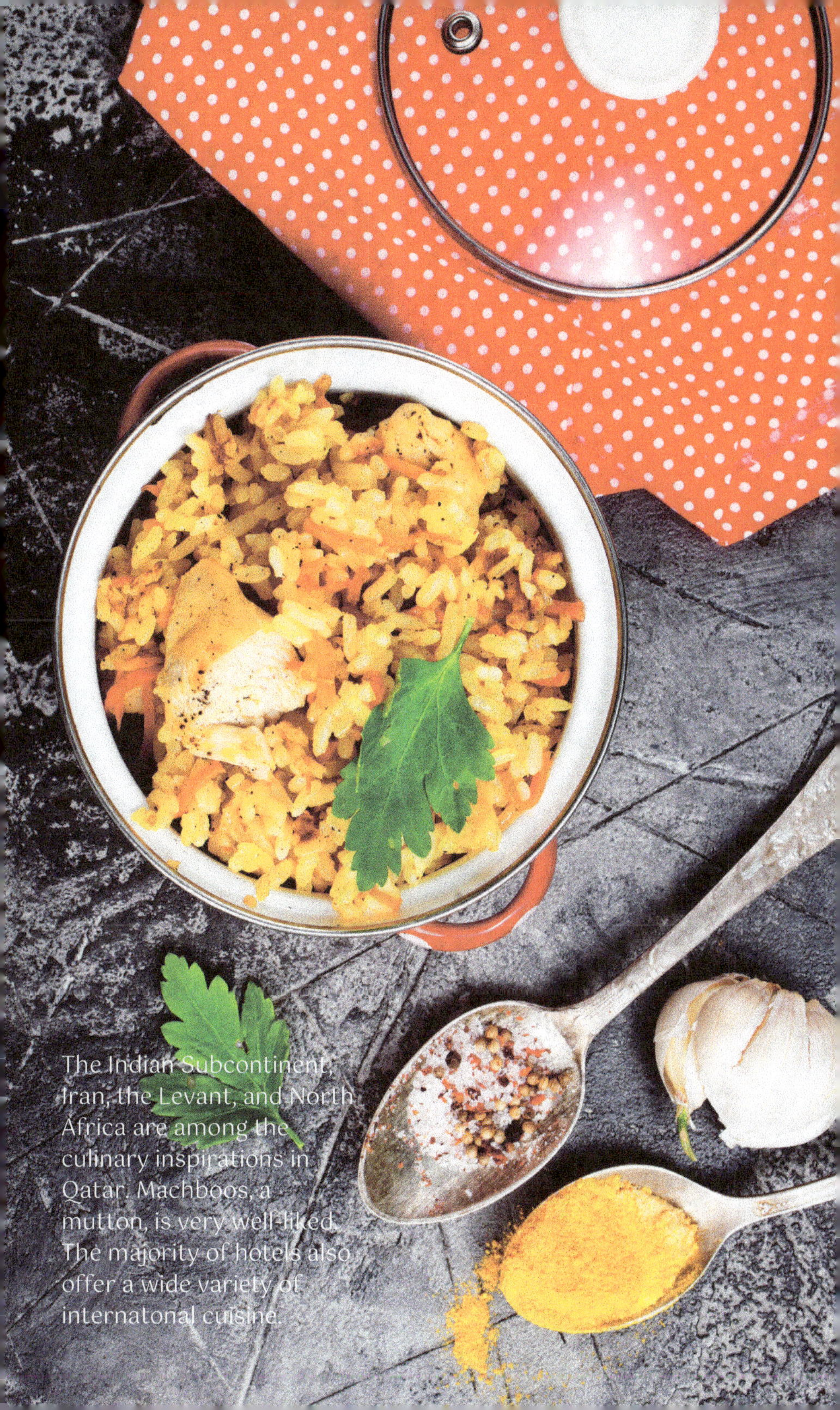

The Indian Subcontinent,
Iran, the Levant, and North
Africa are among the
culinary inspirations in
Qatar. Machboos, a
mutton, is very well-liked.
The majority of hotels also
offer a wide variety of
internatonal cuisine.

DOHA TOWER

The Doha Tower is a 46-story building that was designed by the French architect Jean Nouvel. The building has no central core and is the first skyscraper in the world to use internal reinforced concrete diagrid columns. The façade is a nod to the ancient Islamic design, Mashrabiya, and it is just an incredible building to look at.

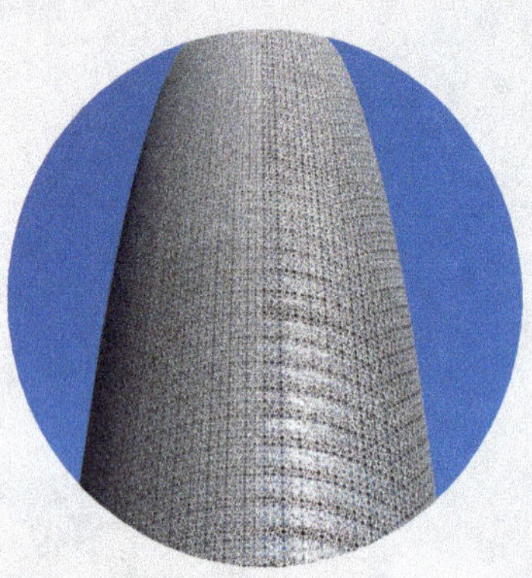

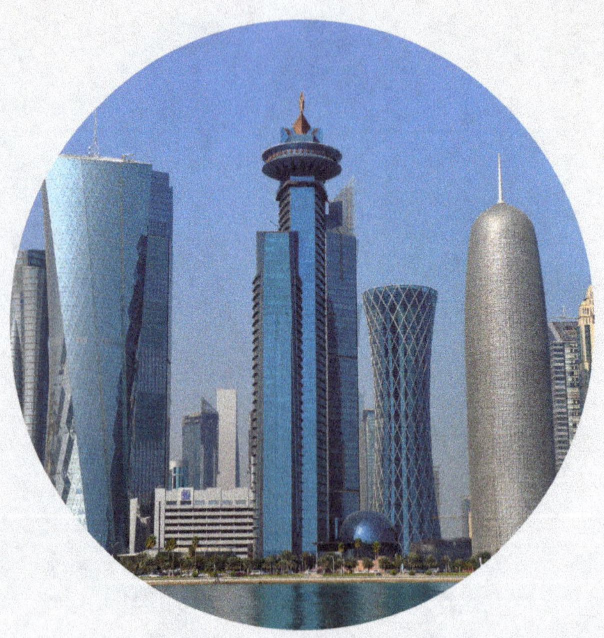

DOHA METRO GUINNESS

The Doha Metro was awarded a world record for the largest number of tunnel boring machines operating simultaneously in a single project. During construction, it was awarded the Guinness World Record for the Construction of a Metro Project.

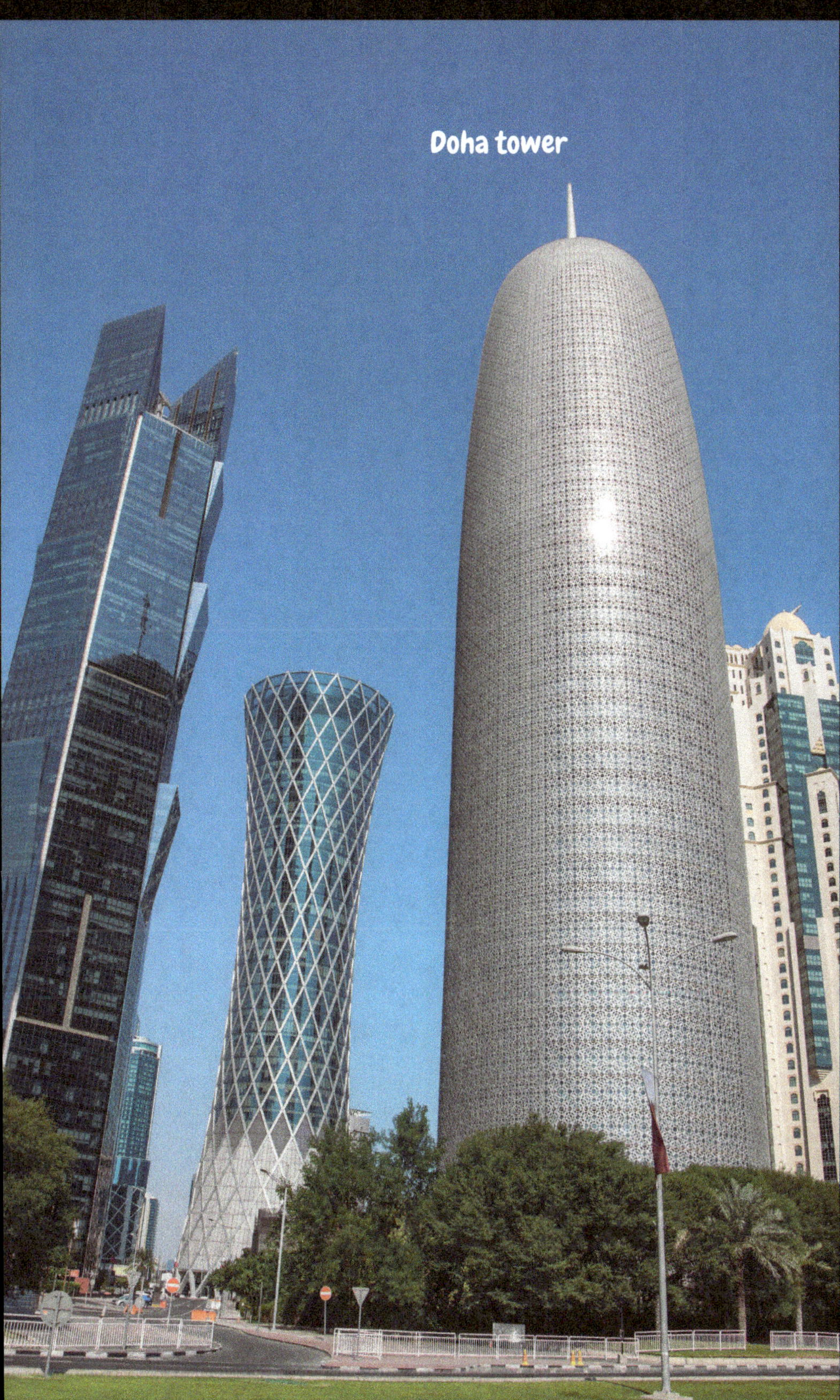
Doha tower

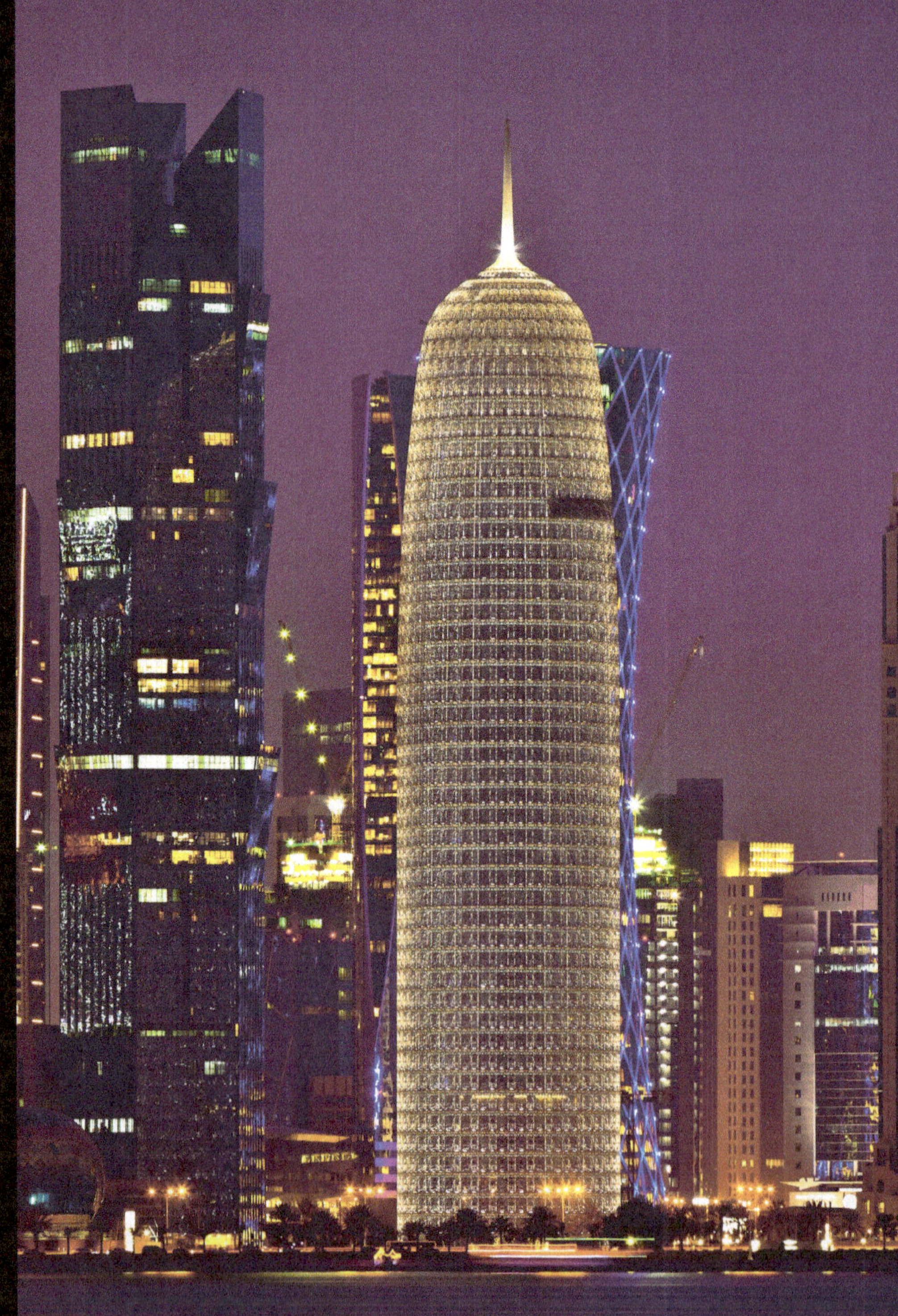

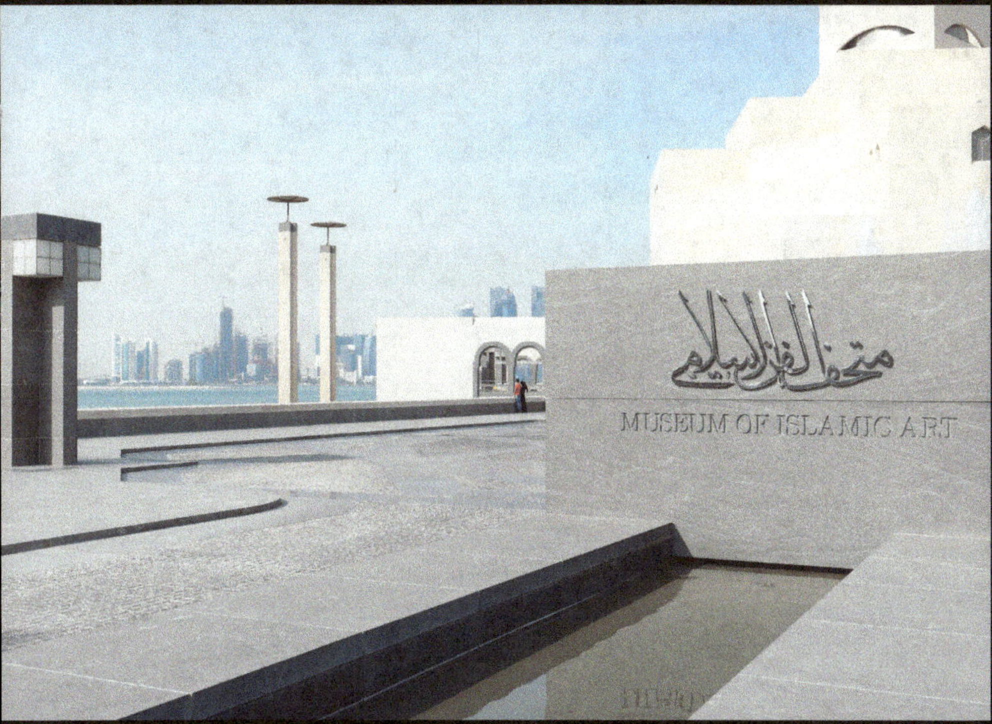

MUSEUM OF ISLAMIC ART

The Museum of Islamic Art (MIA) is one of Qatar's most recognizable structures and is widely known for its diverse collection of Islamic masterpieces from various Muslim countries extending across ages. Thousands and thousands of people walk through its doors every year to see the grandeur and magnificence that make up the Islamic world.

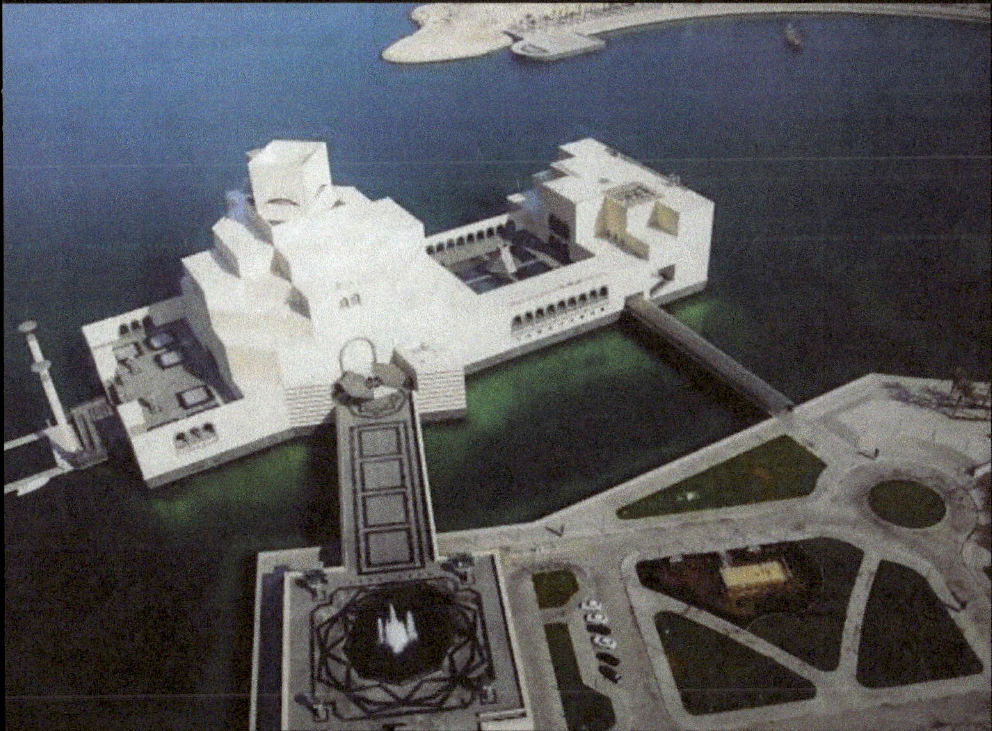

The Museum of Islamic Art (MIA) is one of the most visited attractions in Qatar and was visited by approximately 411,869 people in 2017. MIA was built in the mid-2000s and was opened to the public on 1 December 2008.

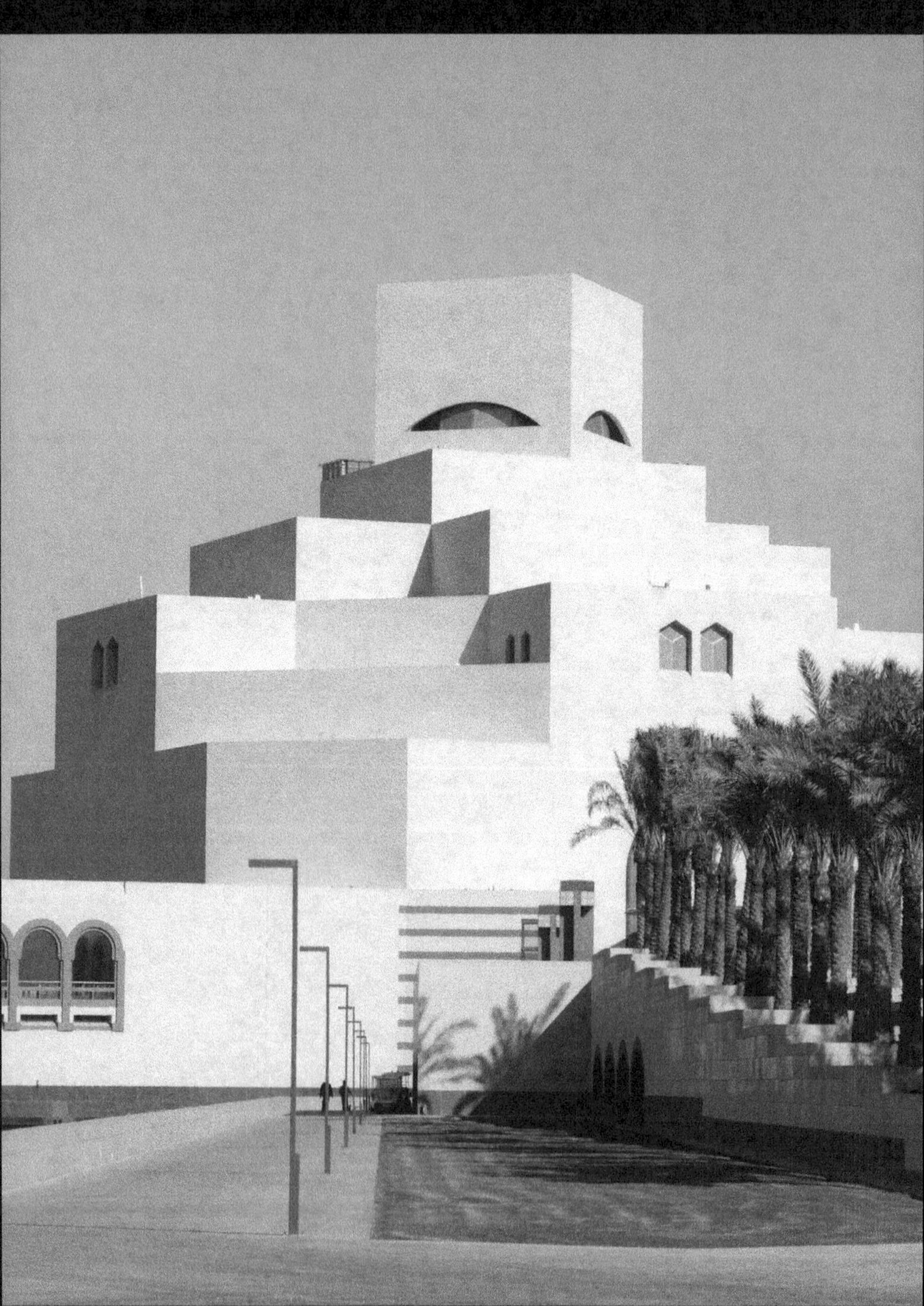

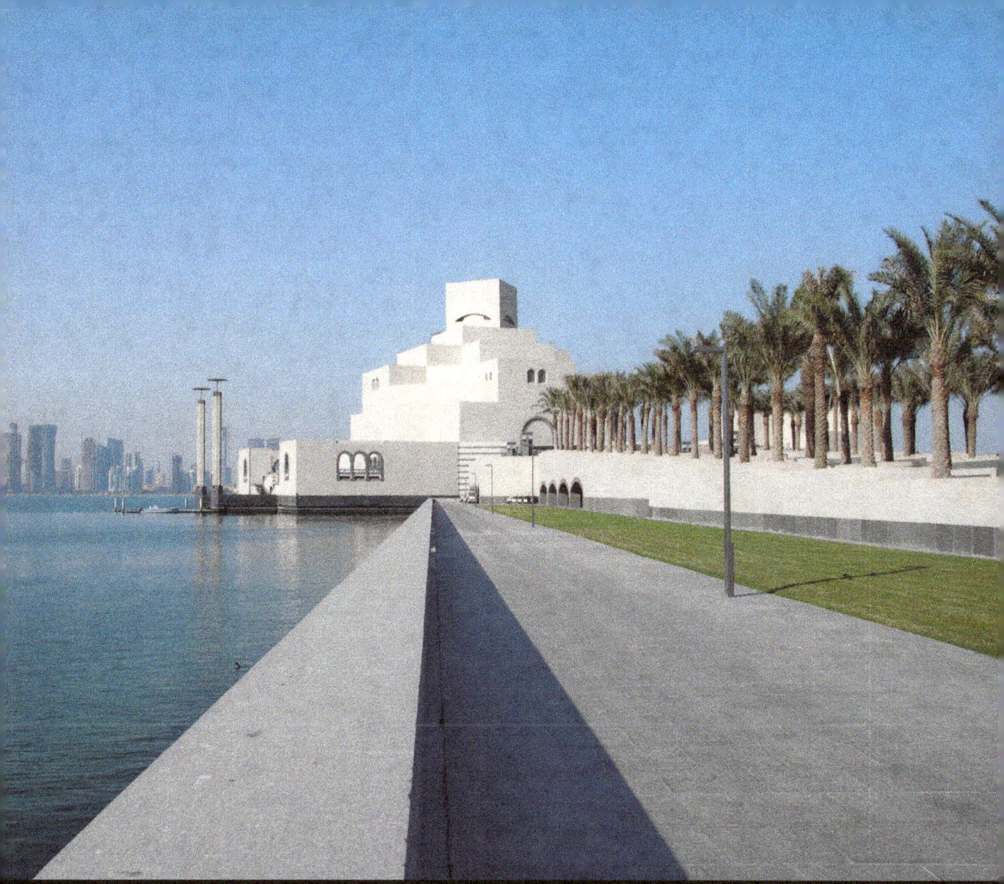

MIA was designed by IM Pei, a world-renowned architect and Pritzker Prize winner, who was 86 and retired at the time he was requested to conceive the look and feel of this beautiful architectural delight. The MIA was built on a stand-alone island about 195 feet away from the Corniche that was specifically fashioned to make sure no structures constructed in the future would stand in its way.

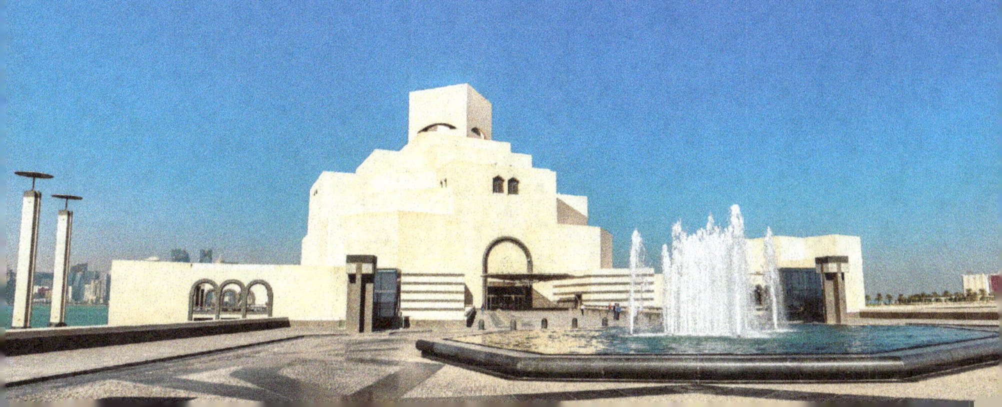

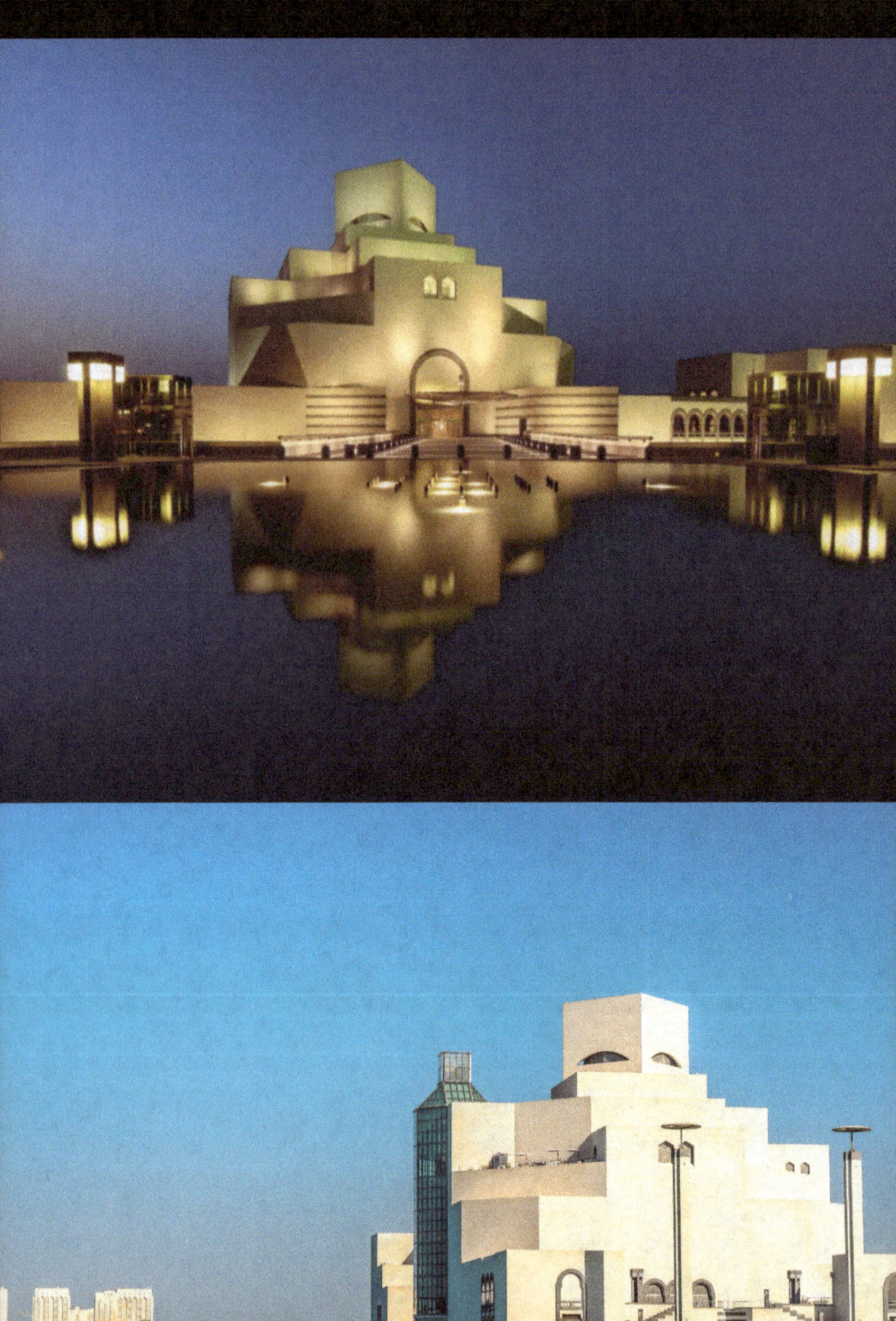

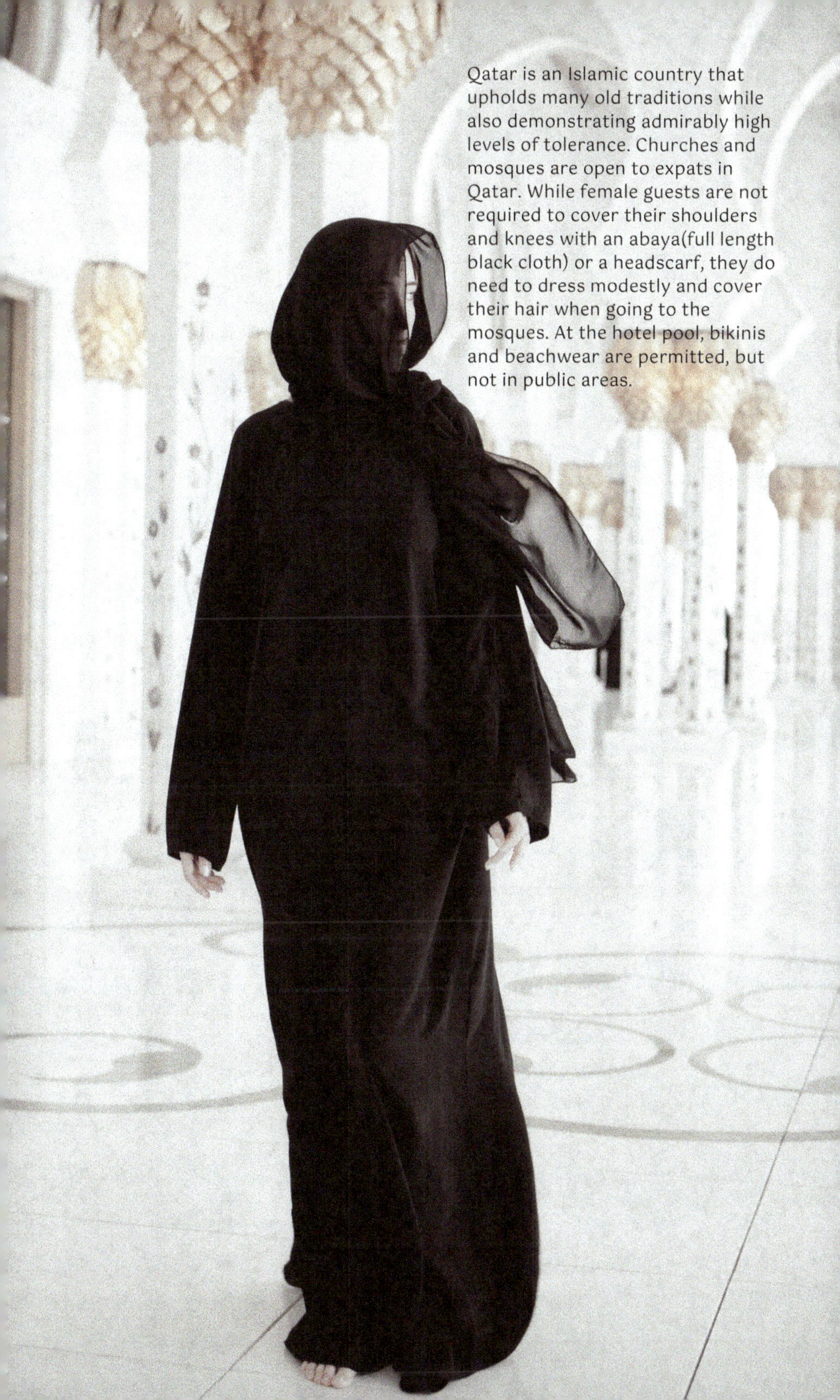

Qatar is an Islamic country that upholds many old traditions while also demonstrating admirably high levels of tolerance. Churches and mosques are open to expats in Qatar. While female guests are not required to cover their shoulders and knees with an abaya(full length black cloth) or a headscarf, they do need to dress modestly and cover their hair when going to the mosques. At the hotel pool, bikinis and beachwear are permitted, but not in public areas.

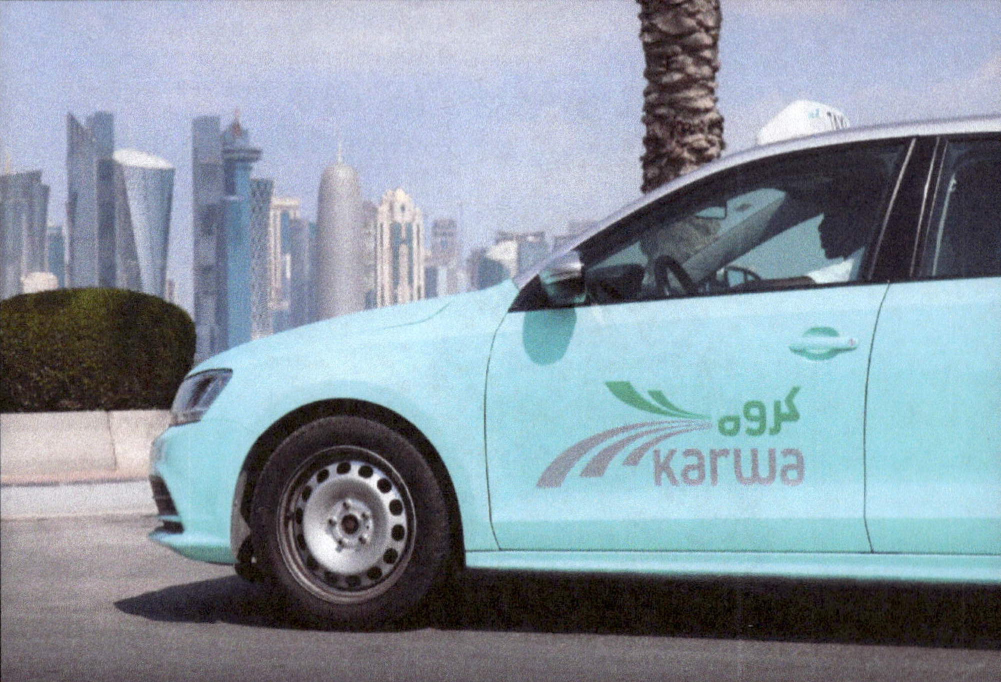

There are several Karwa cabs that are affordably priced. You may contact for service or place an order using the Karwa app. Additionally, ride-sharing applications like Careem and Uber let you rent a private vehicle. It is preferable to reserve an overnight trip if you want to see the breathtaking sunset and dawn in Khor Al Adaid (Inland Sea). Red, Green, and Gold are the three lines of Doha's metro system. The Red Line runs from the city center to Hamad International Airport.

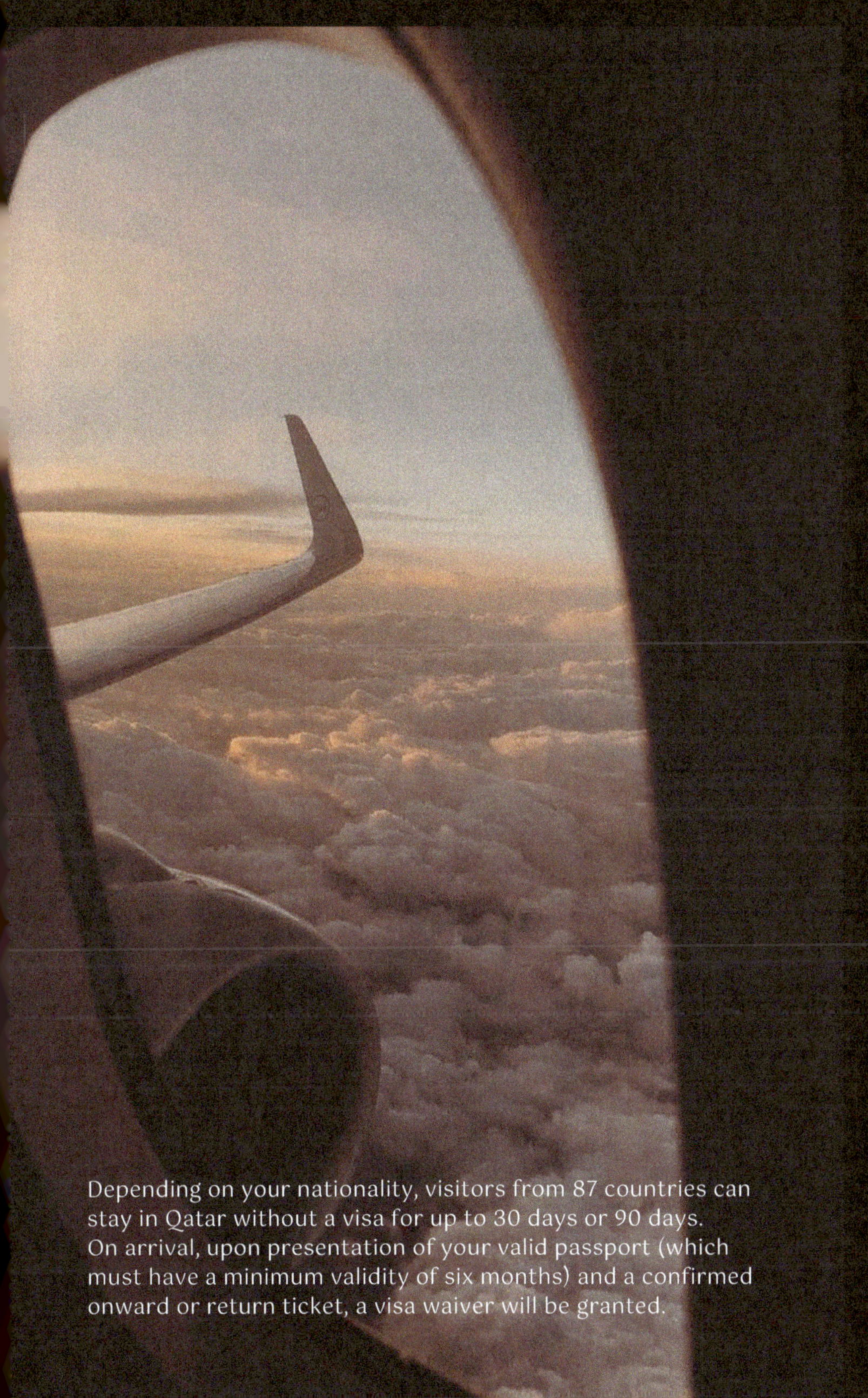
Depending on your nationality, visitors from 87 countries can
stay in Qatar without a visa for up to 30 days or 90 days.
On arrival, upon presentation of your valid passport (which
must have a minimum validity of six months) and a confirmed
onward or return ticket, a visa waiver will be granted.

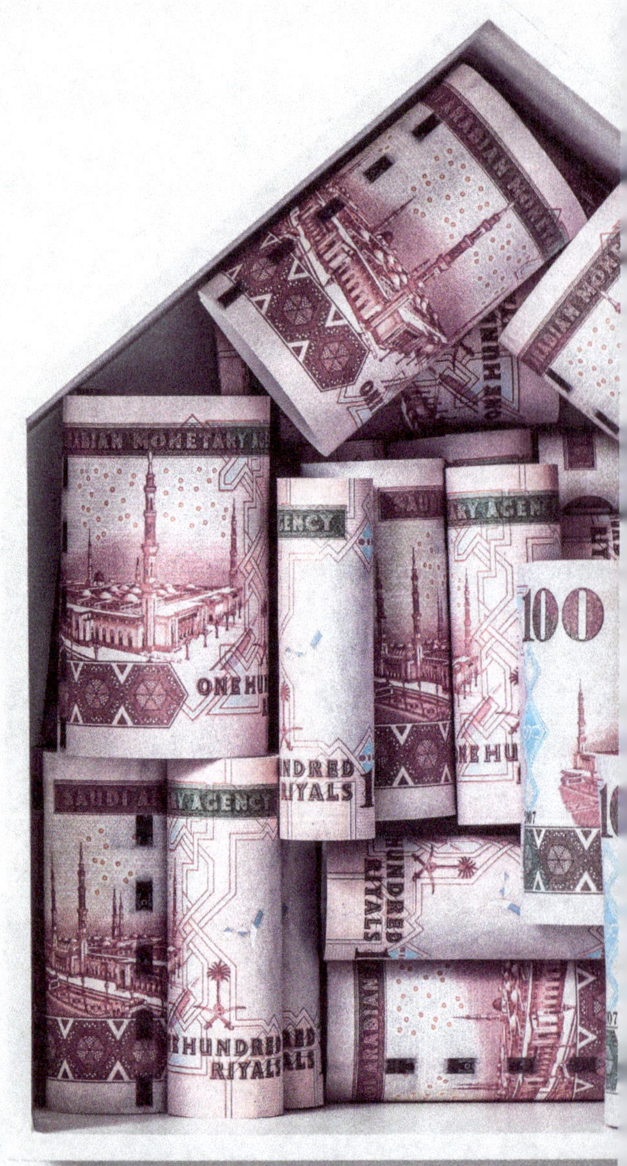

Qatari Riyal is the currency in Qatar. ATMs are widely available so it is easy to withdraw money locally.

Alcohol use in public is not authorized, and alcohol cannot be transported through the airport. Alcohol use, however, is legal in private homes and hotels. The law makes it illegal to be intoxicated in public and disrupt others.

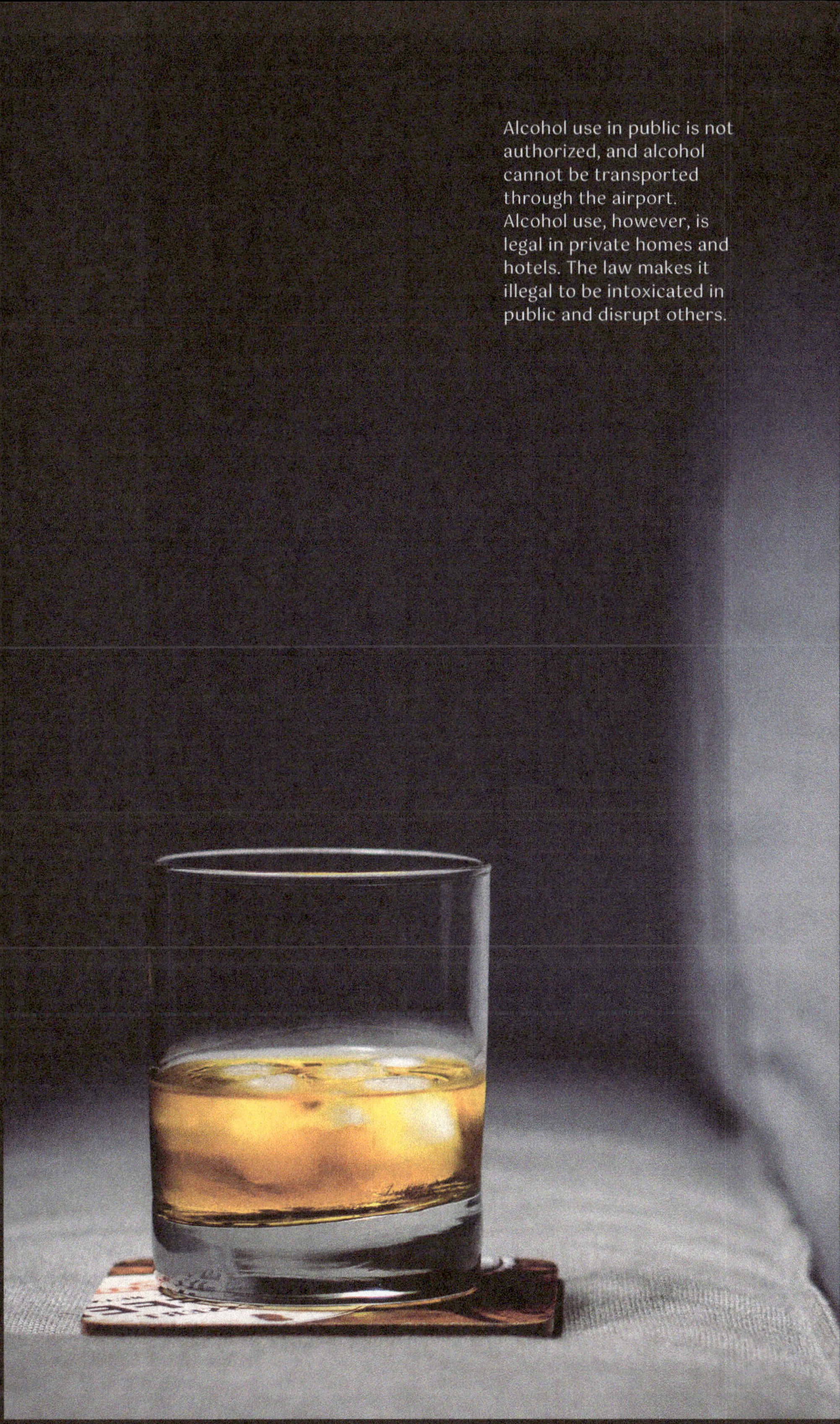

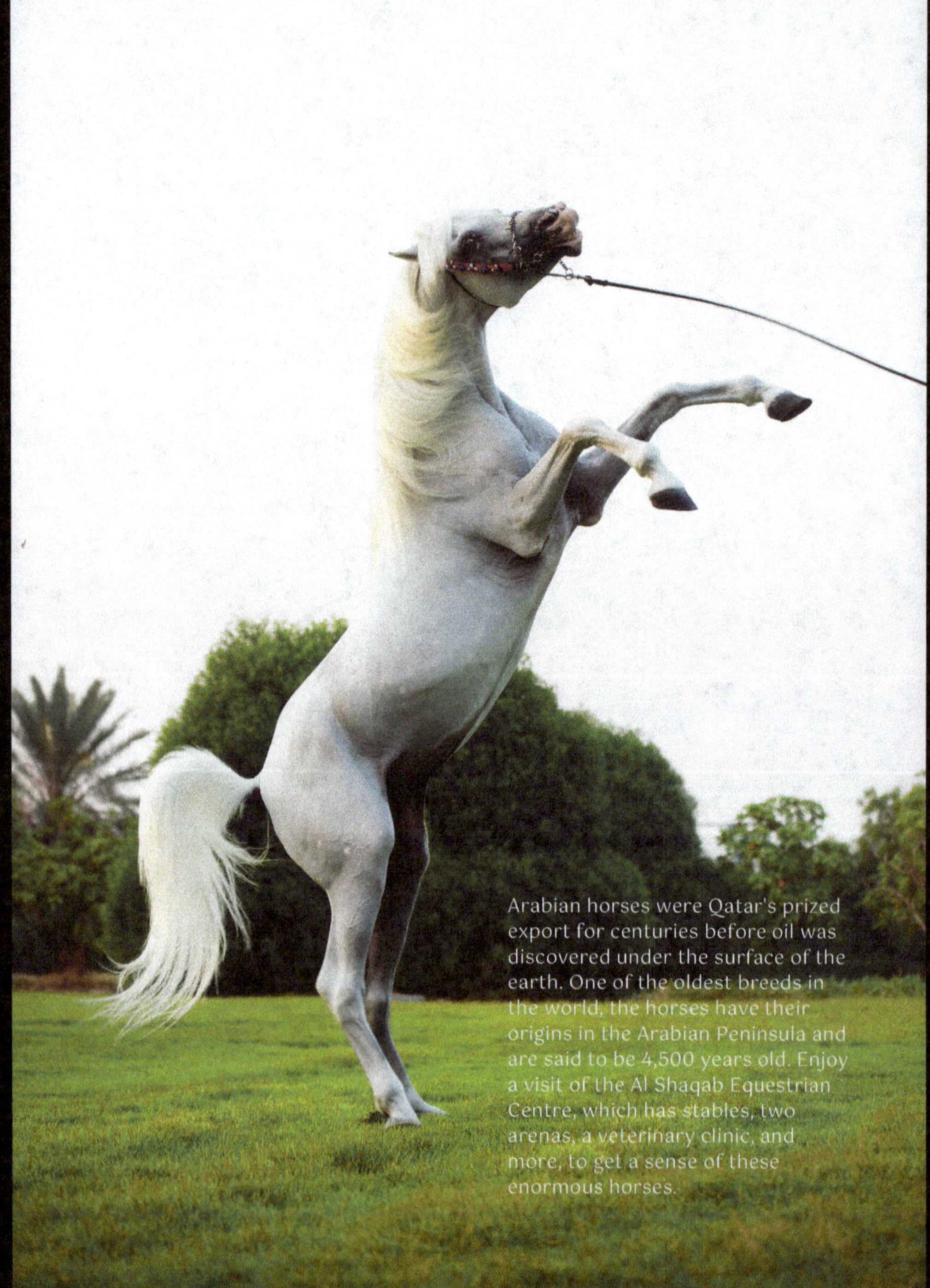

Arabian horses were Qatar's prized export for centuries before oil was discovered under the surface of the earth. One of the oldest breeds in the world, the horses have their origins in the Arabian Peninsula and are said to be 4,500 years old. Enjoy a visit of the Al Shaqab Equestrian Centre, which has stables, two arenas, a veterinary clinic, and more, to get a sense of these enormous horses.

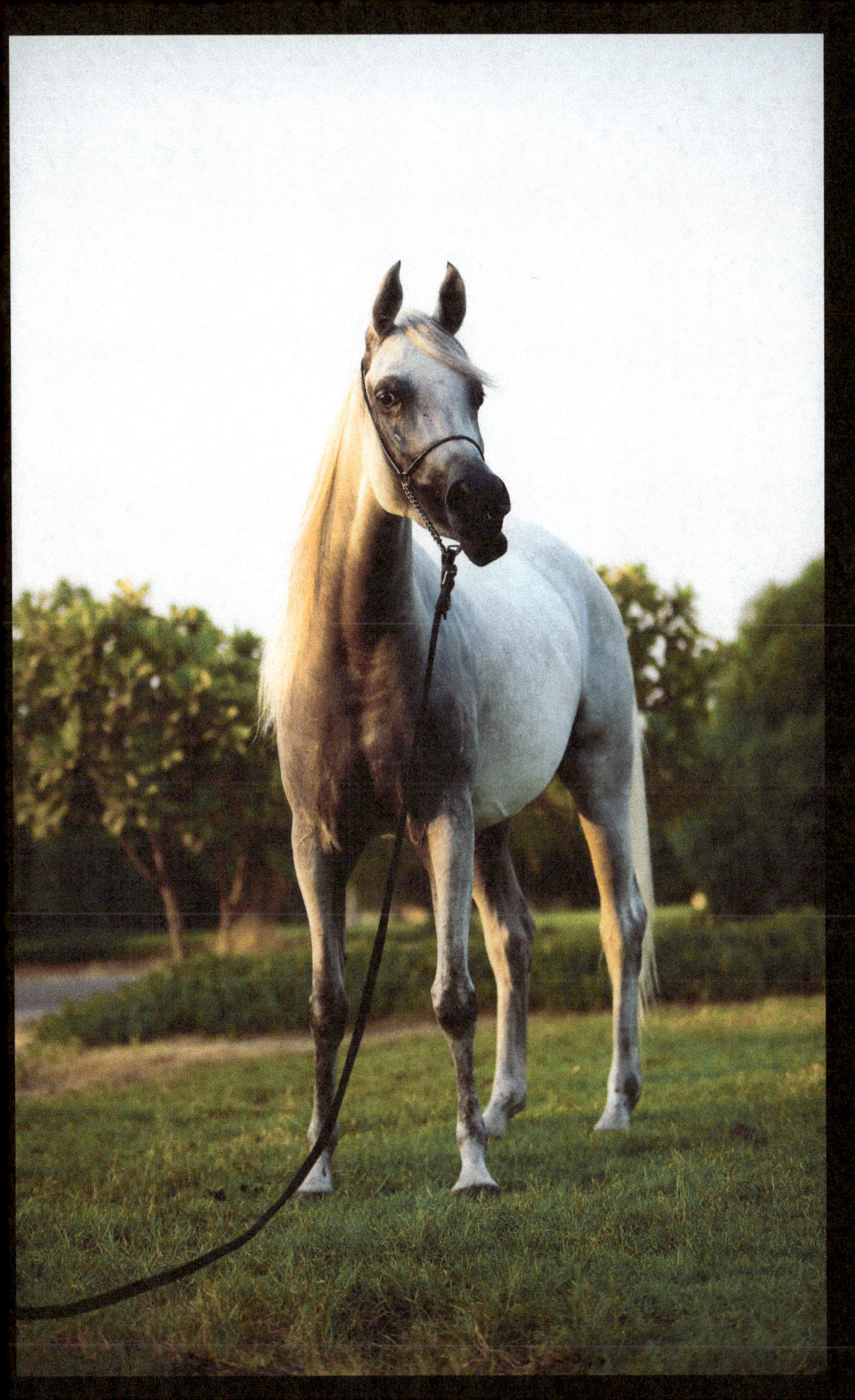

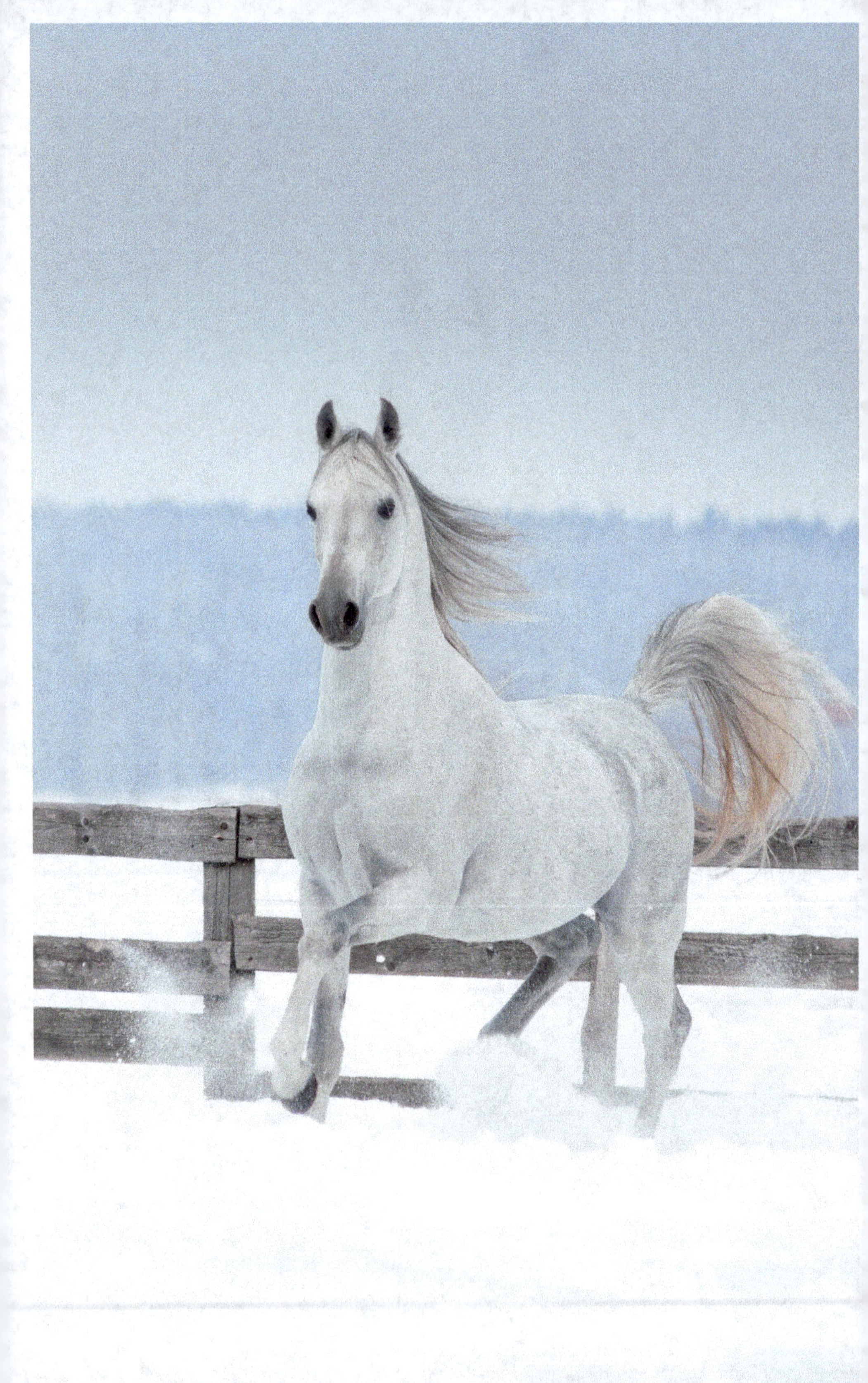

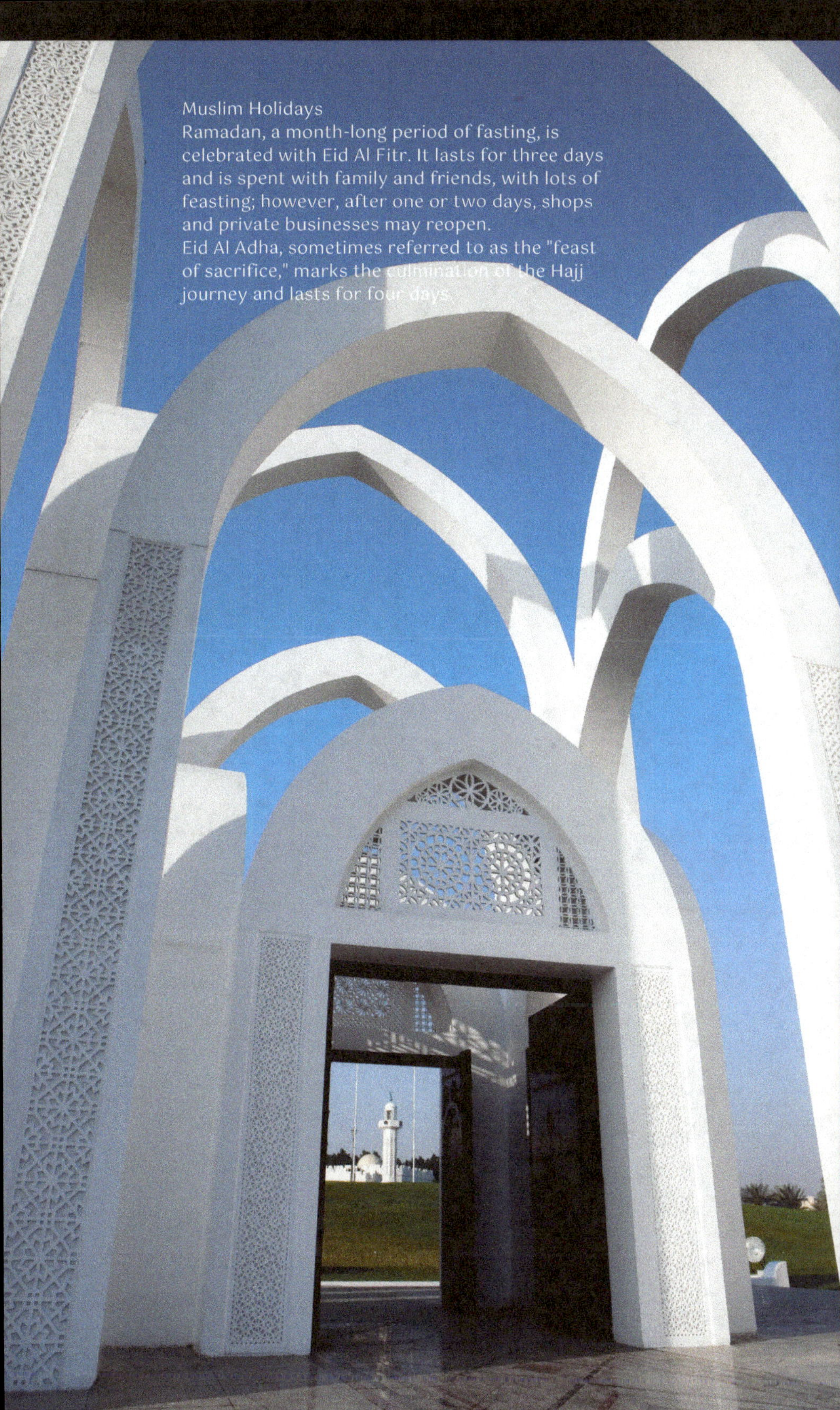
Muslim Holidays
Ramadan, a month-long period of fasting, is celebrated with Eid Al Fitr. It lasts for three days and is spent with family and friends, with lots of feasting; however, after one or two days, shops and private businesses may reopen.
Eid Al Adha, sometimes referred to as the "feast of sacrifice," marks the culmination of the Hajj journey and lasts for four days.

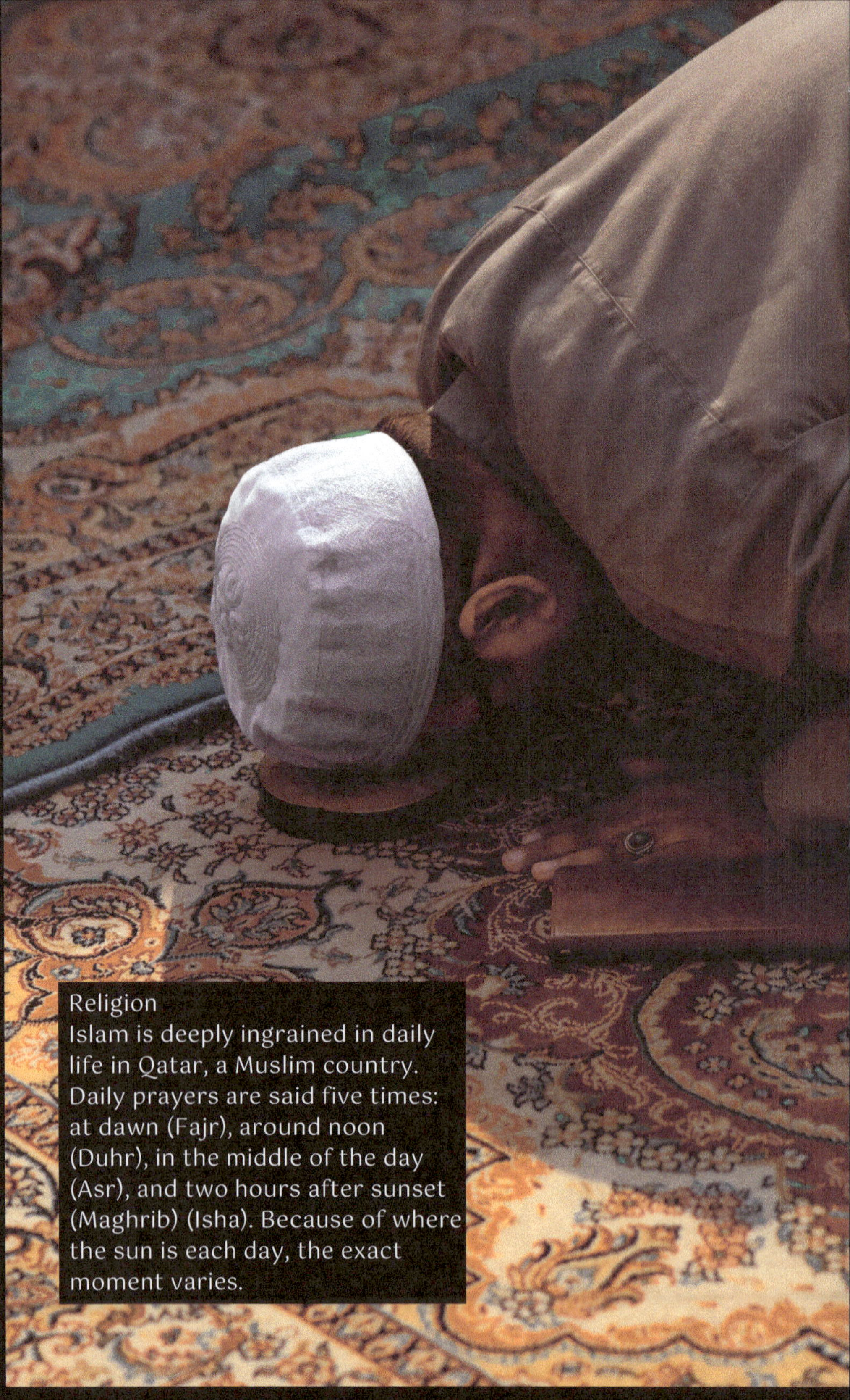

Religion
Islam is deeply ingrained in daily life in Qatar, a Muslim country. Daily prayers are said five times: at dawn (Fajr), around noon (Duhr), in the middle of the day (Asr), and two hours after sunset (Maghrib) (Isha). Because of where the sun is each day, the exact moment varies.

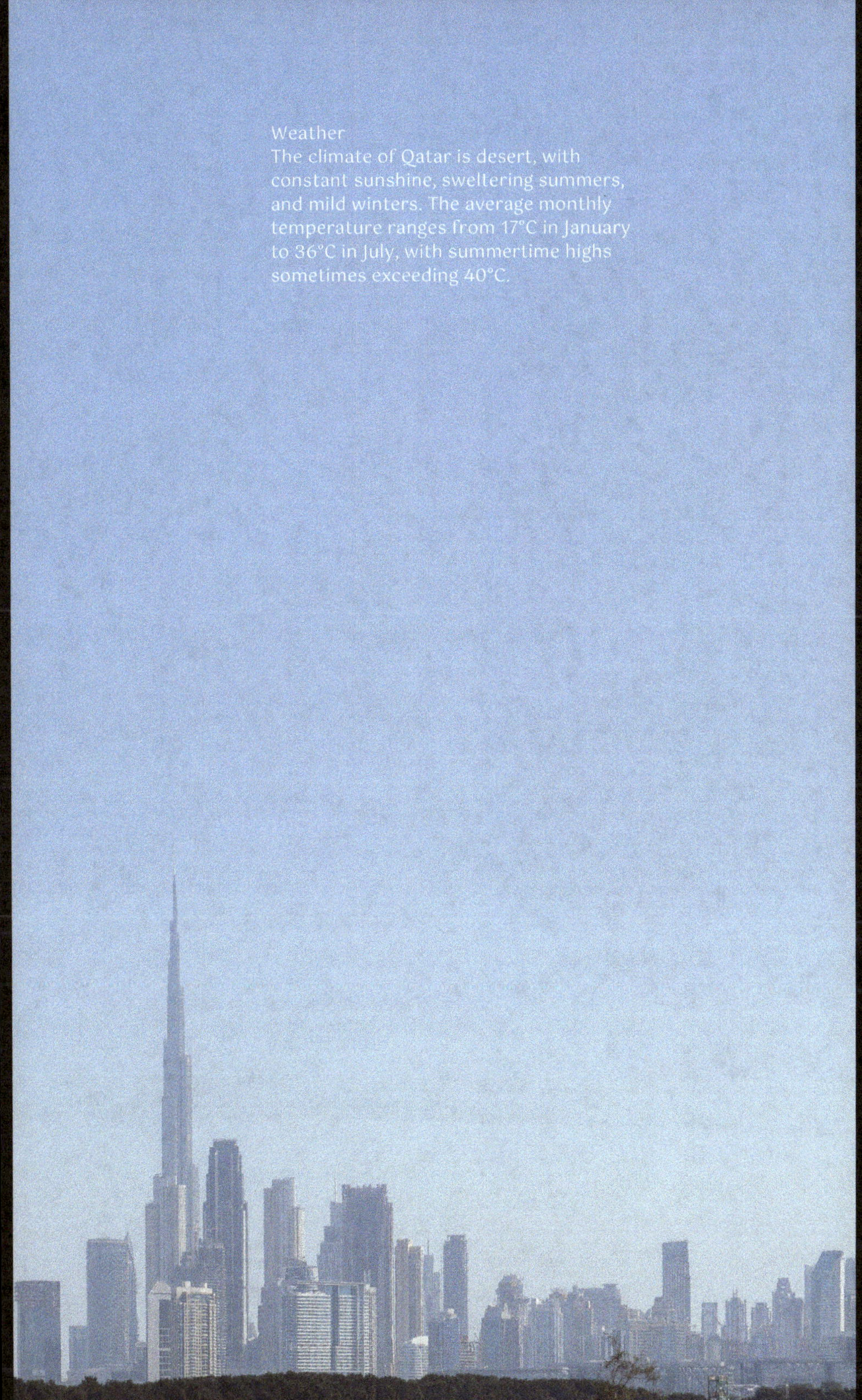

Weather
The climate of Qatar is desert, with constant sunshine, sweltering summers, and mild winters. The average monthly temperature ranges from 17°C in January to 36°C in July, with summertime highs sometimes exceeding 40°C.

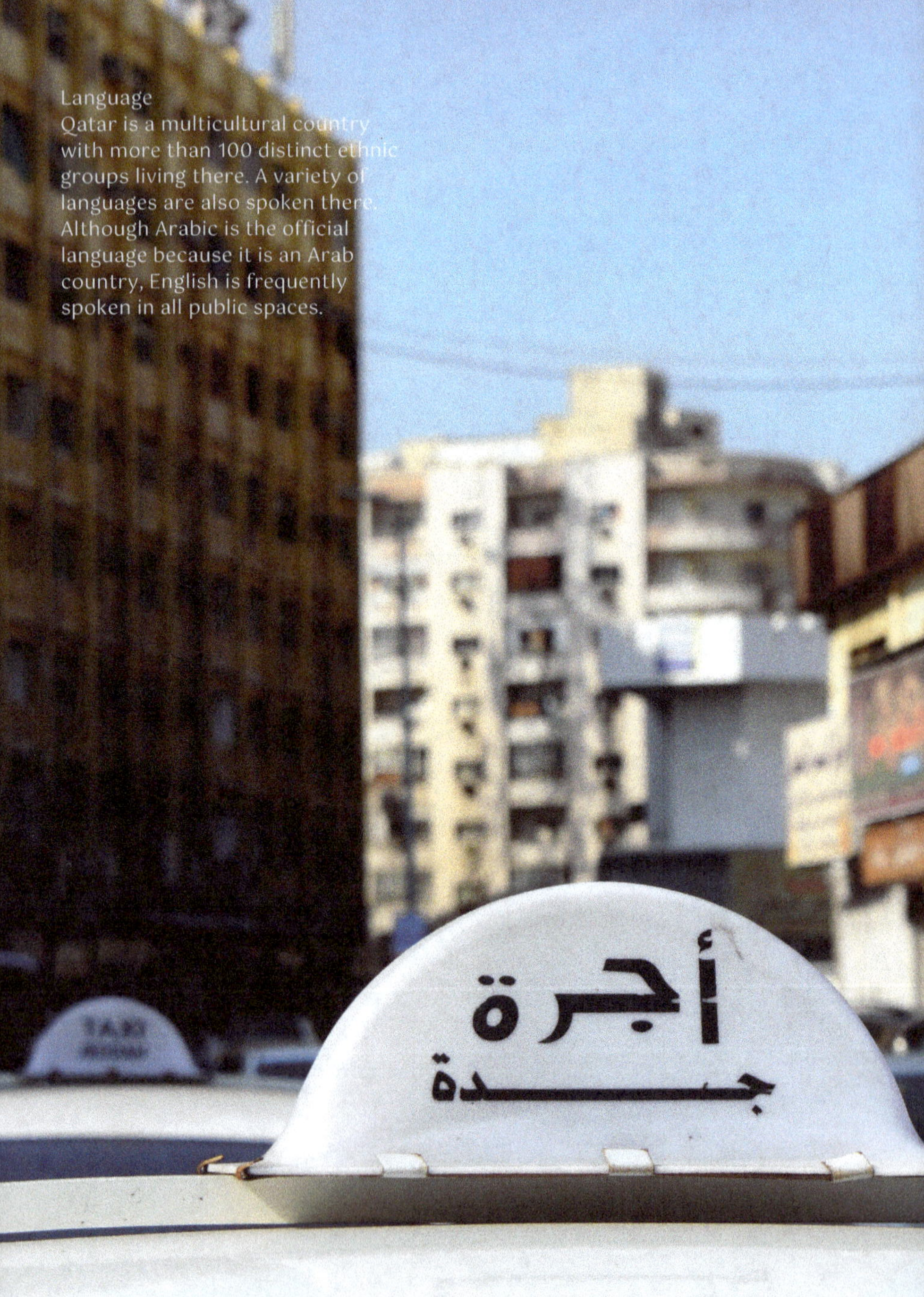

Language
Qatar is a multicultural country
with more than 100 distinct ethnic
groups living there. A variety of
languages are also spoken there.
Although Arabic is the official
language because it is an Arab
country, English is frequently
spoken in all public spaces.

أجرة
جــدة

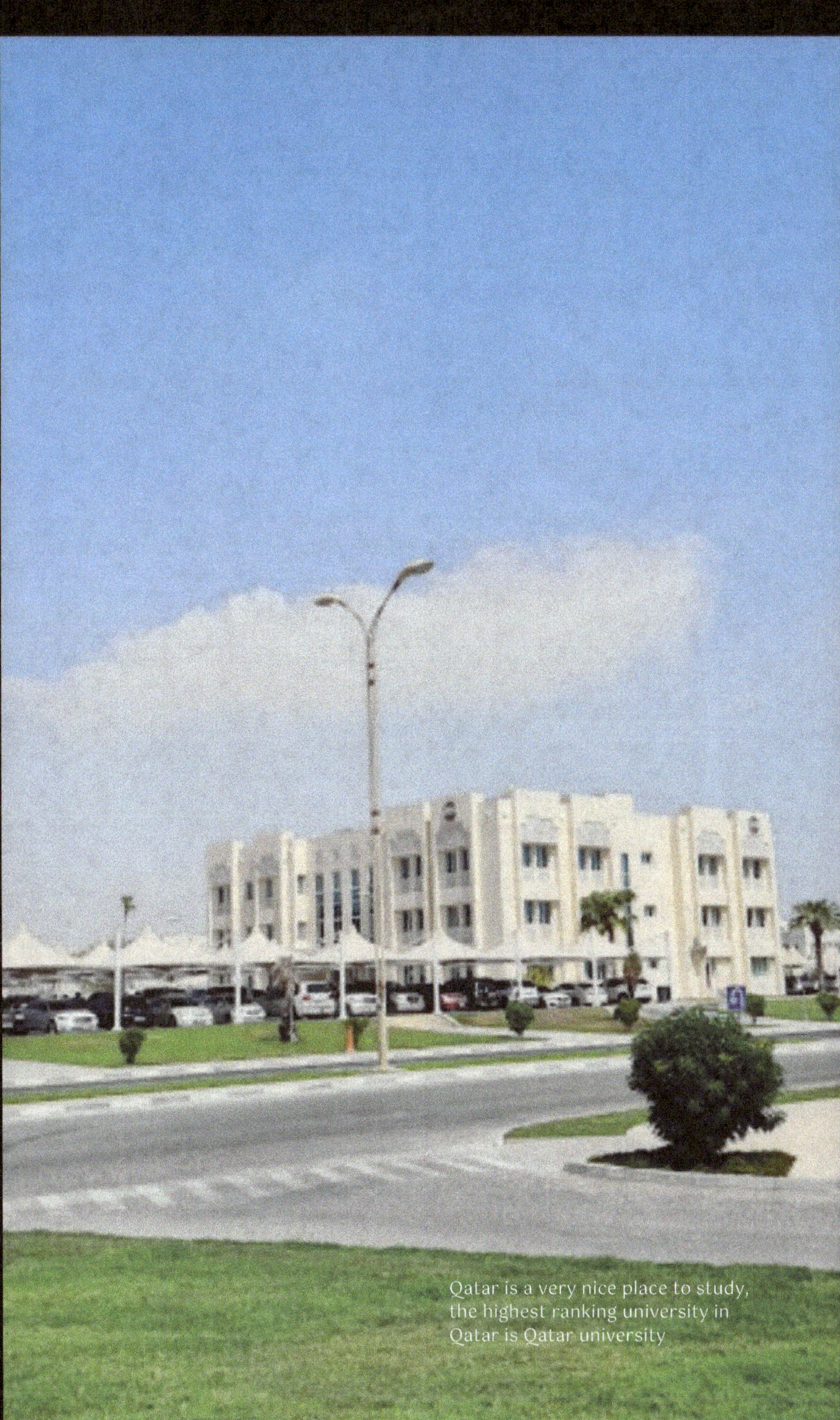
Qatar is a very nice place to study,
the highest ranking university in
Qatar is Qatar university

QATAR

End

I hope you liked reading the astounding facts about Qatar , which are likely to get you eager enough to visit the country soon. Qatar has incomparable elegance and decadence, and during your stay here, you will notice quite a few things that stand out and make you admire the history and culture of the Qatari people.